Exploring Your Life

Also by Mark W. Gura

Blind Faith Vaccine:
Countering Religious Indoctrination

Exploring Your Life
Mindfulness Meditation
and Secular Spirituality

www.inneractionpress.com

www.markWgura.com

EXPLORING

YOUR

LIFE

Mindfulness Meditation
and Secular Spirituality
Full Preview Version

MARK W. GURA

InnerAction Press LLC

Published January 2015 by InnerAction Press, LLC, Duluth, Georgia 30096
Special discounts on bulk quantities of InnerAction Press books are available. For details visit:
www.InnerActionPress.com
Or contact Special Sales Department:
E-mail: info@InnerActionPress.com
Or write to: Special Sales Department, Attn: Mail: Bulk Orders, InnerAction Press LLC,
3780 Old Norcross Rd Suite 103-490 Duluth, Georgia 30096

10 9 8 7 6 5 4 3 2 1

Publisher's Cataloging-in-Publication
    Gura, Mark W.
        Exploring Your Life / Mark W. Gura.—1st ed.
        v. cm.
        Includes bibliographical references and index.
        CONTENTS: Exploring life's meaning, mindfulness meditation full preview version
    and secular spiritualty.
        978-1-939691-09-5 – Softcover
        978-1-939691-10-1 – Kindle
        978-1-939691-11-8 – ePub
        [etc.]

        1. Self-help techniques. 4. Subconsciousness.
    3. Self-actualization (Psychology)—Religious aspects—
    Buddhism. 4. Meditation. 5. Spiritual Life
    I. Title.

    BF632.G87 2015   158.1—dc23
                            QBI13-200001

Printed in the United States of America
Illustrations by Mayfly Design and Vijay K. Chouhan

This book is dedicated to
my meditation teacher, the late S. N. Goenka,
and to the happiness of all beings.

Find meaning in life
Help others,
Attain inner peace
without
Gods (s), gurus, or the supernatural

Contents

The Following bonus chapters and sub-chapters are included in the complete version of the book *Exploring Your Life*:

Your Current State of Being
    Maslow's Hierarchy of Needs
    Explanation of Hierarchical Levels (complete version)
Inner-Actualization
    Life Examples

A Note from the Author

There comes a point in life when some of us ask the questions, "Why am I here?" "What is my purpose in life?" "What is all this for?" We ask these questions because we seek to live a better life. We want to experience less suffering, an ultimate form of happiness—in other words, satisfaction.

Think about those instants when time seems to stop, when you are caught up in the moment, when you feel stillness and satisfaction. Or imagine the feeling that you get when you feel wonder, when you contemplate a single blade of grass covered in morning dew, when you ponder the vastness of the universe with its trillions of stars and countless spiraling galaxies. When we are mindful, we experience this sort of contemplative stillness that is the essence of a spiritual experience, free from faith in mumbo jumbo.

The words "mindfulness" and "wonder" have become popular lately, but what do they mean?

Studies conducted by neuroscientists have shown that when we are mindful, we enter an altered state of consciousness.[93] This is sometimes described as mindfulness, spirituality, or wonder. I call this secular spirituality, but more on this later. Studies indicate that being mindful increases well-being and re-wires our brains so we feel less stress, depression and anxiety.[126]

There are actually two types of mindfulness. The first, spontaneous mindfulness, is the type that we've been discussing, and it just happens without our intent. Purposeful mindfulness, the second type, is enacted intentionally and is aided by a technique that deepens and prolongs the experience. Studies conducted on purposeful mindfulness conclude that it is even more powerful than spontaneous mindfulness. In addition to giving all the benefits mentioned, it also reduces suffering and instills satisfaction.[126]

Another word for purposeful mindfulness is "meditation." But when people hear "meditation," some become uneasy. They wonder, *Are we talking about supernaturalism, New Age practices, religion, Theism, or something unscientific?*

There are also two types of meditation: religious and secular. Both forms of meditation produce some of the benefits mentioned above, but religious meditation uses religious or supernatural concepts, so it is not as universal as secular meditation.

Secular or mindfulness meditation (sometimes referred to as insight or vipassana meditation) uses natural elements such as the breath and the body's sensations. It can be practiced by almost anyone, since it is a psychological technique; perhaps this is why it is even championed by the most ardent of Atheists. Also, mindfulness meditation has been practiced for more than 2,500 years, making this technique older than anything offered by New Age traditions, Christianity or Islam.

My personal experience over the course of the last twenty years shows me that mindfulness meditation produces at least four additional benefits: insight, determination, and equanimity, which increases compassion.

When we are mindful, psychological insights that would normally be locked away beneath the surface level of the mind arise from the unconscious depths. This produces insights that empower our own personal journey in life.

The act of allotting a regular period of time for meditation, despite its difficulties, builds determination. Studies show that the single most important factor for maximizing our chances of success is determination. Determined people are much more likely to succeed in achieving their goals than those who give up when difficulties arise.

As one meditates, one comes to face one's deepest psychological processes. Eventually, one begins to notice that the inner pain subsides. This tends to make us more compassionate. After all, it is when we are in a bad mood and are hurting that we tend to take things out on others. Equanimity also decreases the need to distract ourselves with external diversions such as drugs, alcohol, or any other forms of personal escape.

You will find answers in this book that will challenge you and help you set a course in life, but since these are personal questions, they require a personal commitment to long-lasting change.

Author's Journey

At the age of twenty, I found myself with some leisure time, and this allowed me to think about my life. Outwardly, I seemed successful, but I was unhappy and dissatisfied, disenchanted with the way life was turning out. Previously, my cure-all for everything had been financial success and fun times that distracted me from my suffering. My approach was to live hard, play hard, help others, and leave a legacy, but this did not work for me. Past a certain point, financial success, too, was a diversion. Humanitarian pursuits, religion, partying, even time with friends and family—none of these eased my inner pain.

I was not the only one. I noticed that to some extent most people in our society felt the same way. We spent our lives trying to divert our attention from the inner pain, whether we reflected on this or not. I realized that if I continued to live the way I had been living, without seeking a deeper understanding of my life's meaning, I would one day wake up with regrets, and then it might be too late.

I began by learning about the unconscious mind and received certification in Clinical Hypnothcrapy. I've always been a bit of a skeptic. I try not to accept claims without proper evidence, instead basing my beliefs on facts and considering everything else an opinion or a hypothesis; this led me to seek deeper answers and started me on a three-year journey around the world.

Rather than studying meditation and the world's religions and philosophies from books or at university, I chose the experiential approach, to explore these things first-hand and—if possible—find inner peace.

In India, I sat with Hindu mystics who were considered incarnations of God, and I spent a long time in Jaipur, a region in Rajasthan, India, practicing Buddhist forms of meditation. For about twenty years now, I have practiced vipassana or mindfulness meditation, which is a secular, non-religious form of meditation. I have taken part in and helped facilitate nearly twenty 10-day meditation courses and one 20-day course with S.N. Goenka's international vipassana meditation organization.

At the end of my journey, I realized that I was spiritual,

in a psychological sense, but that I was also an Atheist and a humanist. I see no incontrovertible evidence that God, an intelligent personality who created the world, exists. For me, love, goodness, compassion, spirituality, conscience and honesty are universally human, psychological qualities, not exclusive inspirations from God. I self-identify as a Secular Buddhist—not because I believe the Buddha to be a god or supernatural miracle maker, but because I honor the secular meditation techniques that he created.

I do not have any incontrovertible proof that the supernatural exists, nor do I believe in the mystical explanations of rebirth (reincarnation). If rebirth turns out to be incompatible with the laws of physics, then it will have shown itself to be a myth. Any belief or statement that is not consistent with or corroborated by reason and the best science available should be considered an opinion, and this applies to my statements as well. I am a Secular Buddhist because I take inspiration from some of the Buddha's philosophy and from his methods of mindfulness meditation, which I consider effective, universal, psychological tools that make my life better and lead to personal transformation. I am open to changing my mind about any hypotheses that I hold, as long as proper evidence exists to warrant the change.

Based on my observations, I now believe a balanced inner life requires no faith in religion or belief in the supernatural. People do not need to dedicate their lives to such things to access wonderment, mindfulness and spirituality.

In order to help break free of perceived forms, I now dedicate my life to encouraging the use of reason and critical thinking, teaching and practicing secular meditation techniques that produce happiness from within.

Chapter 1

Happiness

*"Listen to me as if I were speaking to myself.
I'm allowing you access to my inmost self."*
—SENECA, *LETTERS FROM A STOIC* NO. XXVII

This century began ominously for the United States, with a global cyber threat[1] and a cauldron of Middle East contention bubbling over into wars, conflicts and ever deepening fault lines. We were woefully unprepared for the devastating explosions and towers of smoke that rocked the quiet morning of 9-11, and our confidence in being secure an ocean away from the terror in the Middle East was burned away in white-hot flames of unthinkable horror.

Since then, events have led other parts of the world to suffer economic downturns, failed policies, wars, revolutions and uncertainty that affect the lives of hard-working and innocent families, perhaps bringing into question a person's ability to protect what is important to them and making it seem unavoidable for our inner worlds to be influenced by external events. It might seem that there are likely no rains heavy enough to quell the burning and no resolve strong enough to right the wrongs.

While some suffer from external hardships, others are affected by the opposite problem. They are overwhelmed by their own internal psychological processes and thus turn successes into failures, dreams and would-be Self-Actualization into dissatisfaction. They are continually hoping for satiation but never reach it despite their achievement of countless pleasures, projects and fantasies. No matter what they do or how hard they try, they do not fill their empty hearts. Their throats are dry, like those of mariners sailing a cracked boat on a giant ocean dying of thirst although they are surrounded by water.

The good news is that we can overcome our difficulties and take a different course of action. This is a journey that we can share together, that empowers insight and intuitions and reveals answers to the heroic life we long to live.

Suffering: the Problem

> *"To see your drama clearly is to be liberated from it."*
> —KEN KEYES, JR.

The subconscious goal of every being is to escape from its perceived form of suffering. *We are hard-wired to seek survival, but after that, we all want the same thing—to feel good, to have a happy life.* So why do so few people feel good?

One of the main reasons it is difficult to escape suffering

is that we have become accustomed to our stress and misery. How many times have you heard the old saying, "No pain no gain?" I prefer the saying, "Pain is unavoidable; suffering is optional."

Even though we live mostly unfulfilled lives, too many people have stopped seeking to eradicate stressful thinking. We are so calloused by our inner turmoil that we no longer recognize that it is limiting our greatest potential.

This is reminiscent of severe malnutrition, when a person is used to eating a tiny cracked piece of bread with water, and this is his daily condition, to which he becomes apathetic as a survival mechanism. At first the suffering is great, but eventually the pain of hunger becomes dull and he becomes listless, until he reaches the final stage. Then he either fights and survives or fades away.

How then to change this condition? Let us first define our goal.

What does happiness mean to you? Notice that happiness can come from external or internal sources; it can be based on factors that we control or that are outside of our control. We can base our happiness on attaining economic, social, political, or psychological goals. Mostly, happiness means that at any moment you feel at peace, at the center of your life, satisfied, and that this condition is within your control and that it is sustainable and repeatable. How often do you feel this way?

Prevailing wisdom sends mixed messages and sets lofty goals. It tends to say that you will achieve satisfaction if you do what feels good, if you follow your goals and dreams, help others, and if you achieve wealth and fame. But look around you; the world is full of people who have achieved some or all of these things. Are they satisfied?

To make it easier to talk about, for now, let us call any feeling that is stressful or painful "suffering." It manifests unnecessarily, in a number of ways: as discontentment, dissatisfaction, frustration, dread, anxiety, depression, boredom, misery and sadness, or any other bad feeling. The opposite of this, the feeling that we have when all is well, equanimous and centered, is "satisfaction." To discuss the human condition in a way that leads to practical answers, let us put aside any other definitions of these words, at least for the duration of this reading.

People who realize that they suffer and want to find a way to cease their stress share a common predicament. Our endless pursuits of needs and desires cause feelings of both worthiness and worthlessness. Our results are not predictable, our satisfaction not sustained. If you have already achieved some level of success, notice that you probably still suffer, partly because of these inconsistent results. Take a moment to reflect on this: *Will your goals and activities actually bring the satisfaction they seem to promise, or will they leave you wanting more?*

Some still believe that all we must to do in life is to live hard and work hard: develop our talents, raise a family, love others, make a difference, and achieve our social, economic and religious goals, and that passing these checkpoints will bring a serenity and satisfaction that banishes all stress and suffering. Others have seen through this, knowing that while these things are fulfilling and should be done for their own sake, they will not banish the inner dissatisfaction we feel but will merely serve as a temporary diversion from life's ultimate suffering. They know there is a better answer.

Please do not misunderstand me. It is unavoidable and advantageous to pursue and achieve goals, to have nice things, to work hard, indulge in pleasures, love others and leave a legacy, as long as we realize that peace, contentment and satisfaction do not come from achieving external things that change, or from attachment to these things.

Things that change divert our attention from our discomforts, so they seem to work to alleviate suffering, but this is only temporary. But they produce a cycle that is the opposite: the cycle of "the more we achieve, the more we want." The more we want, the more we do. Constant *doing* causes dissatisfaction and even more wants. But what is dissatisfaction?

It is stress, a form of suffering. Is this not the very thing we are seeking to alleviate? If you still suffer, the chances are good that your current way of living will continue to produce the same results. You will continue to substitute one goal for the next and perhaps be unaware that the coming years will be a repeat of the previous, with only a change of scenery. Why is hardly anyone satisfied? Because the problem is not physical; it is psychological.

A Solution

Most people do a fair amount of research before doing mundane things such as buying a car—an object that will last them maybe ten years. They go to the web, ask their friends, read reviews with a skeptical eye and perhaps even ask a mechanic's opinion. But how many research the very thing that is most important—*their own lives*? Why not research the deeper meanings of things and the different possibilities that are available? Study your Life's Trajectory and the mental state that you are creating. Do not resign your fate to hope. Hope is not an effective strategy.

This book is the product of two decades of searching and discoveries. It is designed to help free us from the "empty self," a psychological state of being that is the norm for so many but that ensnares the mind and hinders personal well-being. When life is lived without this greater purpose in mind, it tends to leave us vulnerable to life's changes and disappointments. Therefore, our cause here is to transcend those preoccupations in life that prevent us from achieving inner satisfaction.

The techniques discussed here do not rely on religious practice, faith in mysticism, or supernaturalism. In general, this work strives to help us use the power of the unconscious mind and evaluate our ultimate goal from a rational, historic and scientific perspective. This book reveals the treasure trove of wisdom that lies dormant in your unconscious, *now* waiting for you to unlock its powerful psychological tools and truths. This is for those individuals who have achieved what they have set out to do and now ask, "What's next?" It is also for those who are soul-searching and need to find their own answers.

It is not about how happy or unhappy you are right now. It is about where your peace of mind and contentment come from so when things change, you are still in a positive frame of mind, experiencing inner peace, mindfulness, wonder and satisfaction that continue regardless of the circumstances. We call this state of being Inner-Actualization.

Inner-Actualization provides the ability to draw peace

and satisfaction from within, regardless of the circumstances that surround us. It results in a centered understanding of life's ultimate meaning, a state of mind free from psychological suffering; a state that is not dependent on things that change or disappoint. This gives us a greater purpose, one that is engaged and empowered by inner satisfaction.

Life should be about more than survival, the acquisition of things, the constant striving to satisfy our need for Social and Esteem Needs, and it can be more than Self-Actualization. But this process of Inner-Actualization is not an act of intellectual understanding; it is an inner act, that occurs on an unconscious level and is activated by you, mindfully, from moment to moment. Ultimately, this sort of mindfulness clears the unconscious mind of the hindrances that cause suffering.

Inner-Actualization A state of peace and satisfaction that continues regardless of the circumstances, based on Internal Sources which are not dependent on anything supernatural. Results in a centered understanding of life's ultimate meaning, a state of mind free from psychological suffering. Using Internal Sources and mindfulness to clear the unconscious mind of encumbrances, ultimately eliminating the causes of unnecessary suffering.

Religion Any organized system of spirituality whose core concepts depend on belief in the supernatural or simply as an organized system of spirituality.

Spirituality Used here in a secular, psychological sense to denote a psychological state of being, the innate awareness that occurs when the intellect accesses the Higher Unconscious mind. In the broadest sense of the word, spirituality represents being in touch with our greatest potential.

Chapter 2

Personal Realizations

*"These sons belong to me, and this wealth
belongs to me," with such thoughts a fool is tormented.
He himself does not belong to himself;
how much less sons and wealth?"*
—THE DHAMMAPADA, A COLLECTION OF VERSES.

Modern Life

In the beginning of human existence, when survival was the utmost goal, we had to turn a violent wilderness into a place of relative order and safety. Our self-esteem and personal satisfaction came from survival. Life seemed simple, because it was relatively self-directed and spontaneous. We were not burdened by psychological considerations, the social-cultural baggage of later societies, nor were we beset by mechanistic rules, or well-funded political groups seeking control of commerce and culture. Early people moved in a world that writer and lecturer Joseph Campbell has described as "alive and responsive,"[2] to his spiritual needs. Human beings survived

by acts of individual will, guided by a more direct connec-
tion to their instinctual field of knowledge than we main-
tain today. The mind-set of their day rewarded survival-based
decisions, because survival was then our highest hope. Thus,
survival and actions concurrent with survival were the measure of what it meant to lead a heroic life. The results of decisions were easy to discern as they ended either in pain and
death, or in living, until the next day reloaded the challenges
once more.

Campbell laments, "Now it has become to such an
extent a sheerly mechanistic world."[2] In modern times,
humanity is faced with different challenges. Life is no longer as simple and concrete as it was. Physical survival is no
longer considered a heroic feat, because safety and survival
are now relatively easy to achieve. We now aspire to higher,
more powerful potentials, and this causes us to rely more on
our intellect. Unfortunately, frequent use tends to overload
the intellect, and this creates psychic wounds, something
that early humans probably did not experience.

Today, our conscious mind is bombarded with multi-
media content and a whirlwind of information. And beyond
the thousand-fold distractions to our consciousness, we
must add the "fear factors"—some intentionally created by
government and business change agents—that unleash the
torment of uncertainty and foreboding at the primal level of
our unconscious.

Our contemporary world-view has been distorted by the
message that happiness is dependent upon external powers and institutions. This can lead to institutional thinking
and acceptance of diminished, tightly controlled individual
rights. Not only do we stop thinking like heroes, *we barely*

have a true identity of our own. Therefore, a new form of heroism is now required.

Once we have managed to sustainedly fulfill our basic needs for survival, the next heroic step in our development is to face the ultimate challenge, to look within to that place that *is* deep and filled with pain and mystery. The path to inner satisfaction is a heroic destination because it is a journey to the inside of the unconscious, the place where our demons, illusions and desires dwell and cause us misery and mischief. It is selfless and brave to crawl down into the deep, to face and vanquish the stress and suffering that makes people do desperate and miserable things. Knowing the nature of your identity and the power of your individual sense of self is the key to understanding what makes you happy and satisfied.

Personal characteristics form early in life. What we absorb during childhood often stays with us for the rest of our lives, so let me share a few insights from my own "inner scrapbook" of growing up, the better to illustrate how your own formative years set you on your path.

An Inspiration to Change

Even though I have not felt extreme physical suffering, I have experienced struggles in my life that seemed formidable to me. My family and I escaped Communist Poland to seek a better life. This forced us to start all over in new lands that promised hope but required toil and sacrifice. This aggravated my own struggles in school, in life, and in trying to be accepted socially. Living in one place can be like living in a protective cocoon, albeit sometimes with a myopic view.

But growing up in new places, among new cultures and lan-
guages, absent old-time friends and family members can be
a challenge, even though this challenge gave me a unique
perspective on the lives that we lead.

Some children are able to buffer the pains of life with
talent, luck, or charisma. I had none of these in any great
degree and did not possess any extraordinary personal characteristics that could give me any sizable advantages. My
biggest challenge was also my greatest benefactor; it kept
me alert to life's possibilities. Because I lived in different
countries when I was young, I was unable to hide underneath the protective blanket of geographic stability. Travel
often exposes the veneers under which humanity hides its
delusions. Since I was always aware of my inner pain, this,
more than anything, probably caused me to ask some of the
deeper questions that we are now discussing.

Even though my life did not start heroically, nor in any
inspired way, looking back on it, perhaps Poland was an
inspiration to me. After all, it is the land of snow and sun-
light, castles and cathedrals, steppes and forests. And it has
a long history of revolutionaries and powerful thinkers, who
against great odds gave birth to pivotal world change.

I was taught from a young age to have faith and to believe.
The unspoken promise seemed to be that God would solve
all problems and that faith would alleviate life's sufferings.
But for me, this promise went unfulfilled, especially when I
left things to fate.

Poland has been a Christian country since the tenth century. In 1683 Polish King John Sobieski III stopped Muslim
and Ottoman forces at the Battle of Vienna.[4] This battle was
so important to the preservation of Christianity in Europe

that he's now called the *savior of European Christendom*.[5] In more recent history, the Catholic church, along with Polish Pope John Paul II, helped the country regain its freedom from Communism. Then again, Poland is also the birthplace of Nicolaus Copernicus, who championed astronomical science over entrenched religious dogma, and of Madame Marie Skłodowska-Curie, who is now acknowledged as the *mother of atomic physics*. Nevertheless, the majority of the population, those who were not heartfelt communists, freethinkers, or radical philosophers, simply *did not question* belief in God, Jesus or the church.

I witnessed unquestioned faith close-up in my family. I remember putting on my wool coat and galoshes and walking with my grandfather across the park to Sunday mass, a light snow falling across the city. Just a few blocks from our flat towered a gothic-looking cathedral that seemed to overwhelm even the factories that once made Lodz a center of industry. I have heard that there were even centuries-old mosques and synagogues across the city; no doubt they too cast their shadows on their faithful.

The monuments of established religion loomed over me in every direction, and it was in this snowy cityscape that my grandfather talked with me about what religion meant to him. A small question I might ask about a candle or a statue could prompt my grandfather to explain why the Madonna watched over the prayer railing, and how she blessed young couples leaving their marriage coins. I learned that the rites and rituals of our Catholic church were deep inside the heart of my country, city and family. That was good enough for me, and I too, *believed*.

When I studied the Bible, I internalized its teachings. I

accepted its lessons as fact. I did my best to follow the commandments. I believed as a child believes, openly and without question, but God did not show Himself.

By the time I was old enough to go to school, I looked everywhere to see God. Did He watch us from the Gothic turrets of the great cathedral in Krakow, resting with gargoyles, lions and dragons? Did He look up at me from the bottom of Morskie Oko Lake in Zakopane? Did He listen to my mother and great-aunt argue late at night in grandmother's kitchen, about moving to Sweden to join my father, hoping I was asleep and out of earshot? Did He sit quietly on His cloud, while the bully on the soccer field repeatedly tripped boys from the younger form as they ran across the goal line?

Some might say that I had no reason at all to feel stress. In a physical sense, this might be true. My suffering was not physical, but do we not all suffer? Since I was especially aware of suffering, I felt it more than most. I even remember asking God to give me unconditional happiness. Why not? If God loved me personally, why did He not personally intercede and help me?

Looking back at it, it is so easy to idealize childhood, to shrug off feelings and hurts and to label our experiences as normal, or even to be inured to our pain and to see it as unalterable, but in later years, I realized that most human beings felt the same sort of suffering. In fact, most grow accustomed to it, not realizing that we are suffering needlessly.

Sure, during all those years, I felt my conscience stir. I felt different reactions in my mind. Some people say that this is God, or Jesus, or Allah talking to us, but it is just as likely that these are the reactions of the mind, mere psychological and mental phenomena.

We invent and interpret what our feelings mean based on existing beliefs. Therefore, if you believe in Jesus, the tendency is to explain your mental phenomena as Jesus talking to you. If you believe in the god Zeus, you will think you are having an experience with Zeus. I wondered if facts proved our beliefs, or if our beliefs were no more than assumptions forged by will into something even more powerful—convictions.

Even though I gave all my faith and love to God and Jesus, my suffering continued. Accepting Jesus into my heart was not a permanent fix. Sure, faith brought some satisfaction and peace sometimes, but this was only temporary. Perhaps I expected too much from religion. After all, cessation of suffering is not supposed to be the purpose of faith-based religions. According to what I have read in the Bible and the Koran, the ultimate goal of God-centered religions is to serve God, not for God to serve humanity. Theism promises the *potential* of heaven, but only after death.

Geographic Shifts in Perception

One day when I was in the first grade, as we were eating breakfast, my mom announced that we were moving from Poland to France. My family wanted to get away from the stifling communist regime that was controlling Poland at the time and to seek better economic prospects. I was excited at the idea of travel and new adventures; on the other hand, I was sad to leave my friends, family and the place where I grew up.

Paris was somewhat similar to my city of Lodz, except that it seemed two or three times larger and thus busier. Since it was the capital of a nation, it had the best that France could offer. I loved its art, the old buildings and shops, the green parks and throngs of people. It was overwhelming and exciting. The ancient architecture and monuments inspired me. The outdoor markets, exotic sights and multitudes of people made me feel more alive. The French people were great and made us feel welcome. I began to really like the city, but I noticed that here too, my suffering persisted.

You would have forgiven me for thinking that all this adventure and excitement would alleviate the dissatisfaction inherent in the human condition, but no matter where I lived or what adventures my brother Steven and I shared, the distractions of a different geography did not relieve or remove my inner suffering.

Perhaps I had not learned my lesson; less than a year after moving to Paris, my family announced that we were moving to the United States, and I was truly excited. Landing in Houston, we exchanged the gilded glamour of Paris and a warm European summer for the blast-furnace heat of Texas. When the airport doors opened, a wall of humidity and heat hit me in the face. I knew I was no longer in Paris. The dangers and excitements of an ancient capital were replaced by the dangers of going mad from boredom in suburbia.

I realize now that had I lived in only one place all my life, I might have accepted traditional ways of seeing, but living in different countries made me realize that most beliefs are relative and are based on what we are taught by our culture.

This was one of my first conscious insights about Inner-Actualization. Life is a mixture of pleasure and pain, and most people seek to maximize the pleasure and minimize the pain. Everyone I knew seemed to be plagued by the same problem; pretty much no one I knew was satisfied, no matter what people had or did. Even though all their paths and achievements promised satisfaction, none of these worked. Everyone still suffered, and I realized their *method* of escaping suffering *was to continue doing what they had always done*—and what their parents had always done—one generation after the next.

Our pleasures bring us comfort, but they do not make us continually satisfied. That internal tension you feel, even now, behind all your activities, is going to continue until you do something about it. If you use internal tools for being serene, then you will be in control of your serenity. If you depend on Externals, your happiness will depend on things that change.

Because of this, by the time I ended my teenage years, I was faced with an existential crisis: I did not know who I was or what I was supposed to do. I did not know what all this was for.

Ask yourself, "How do I achieve serenity? How do I alleviate the stress and inner turmoil that accumulate and turn to suffering? Is the methodology that I use an Internal Source that is under my control?"

Unconscious Mind The automatic mental processes of the mind, usually referring to any activity in the mind below the general threshold of conscious awareness. Serves as an autopilot for the body and controls our most important biological processes behind the scenes. It is also a source of insight, will, imagination and inner peace. Here the terms unconscious and subconscious are used interchangeably, nor is it associated with any particular school of psychology.

Negative, Positive, Realistic In this book, we will touch on topics that deal with the harsh realities of life. To make more informed decisions, it is important to consider these positions, not in order to embrace pessimism, but to view reality more realistically or pragmatically. Optimism and positive thinking can lead to optimal outcomes as long as optimism is not used blindly. Insights arrived at in this way are hard-won, but they do require the use of reason, critical thinking and the ability to view subjects from many diverse points of view.

Chapter 3

Your Current State of Being

*"Your work is to discover your world and then
with all your heart . . . give yourself to it."*
—THE DHAMMAPADA.

Thousands of years ago, in ancient Greece, the words "Know Thyself" were displayed prominently on the stone walls of the temple of Apollo at Delphi.[7] Ancient Greece was the fountainhead of wisdom in that region of Europe, and it inspired and continues to inspire people all over the world. This particular message concerning the understanding of one's self was deemed so important that it was displayed in the forecourt of the main temple—so everyone could see it. Why is this message so important?

Knowing what you want and where you are in life in relation to your ultimate aims is the starting point for getting what you want, but there is a deeper knowing that is even more important. I call this "Your current state of being." To truly know these things, it is essential to know oneself, one's goal, one's heart—the good and the bad—and especially one's unconscious mind. Having access to the depths of our heart and the ability to control the mind leads to action, and achievement *aligns us with our utmost purpose in life*.

Perhaps this is why the admonition to "know thyself" has been attributed in some form to most saints, sages, secular philosophers and to just about every religion and spiritual path. It is found in the words of Jung, Maslow, Freud, Socrates, Jesus, the Buddha, Pythagoras and many others. Thousands of years later, humanity still deems important. It is arguably the most important directive that one can achieve, because it leads to life's utmost purpose—inner peace.

So, how do you "know thyself?" Who are you? Who are you right now?

Pioneers in the field of psychology, such as Alfred Adler, Sigmund Freud, Carl G. Jung, Milton H. Erickson, Carl Rogers and Abraham Maslow each left an imprint on how we measure who we are and how acceptable or unacceptable our lives are at a given point in time. The core tenets of Inner-Actualization were developed in direct response to a widely accepted (but not entirely successful) belief system known as self-actualization developed by Maslow and made popular by humanistic psychologists such as Rogers.[8]

To understand how basic and secondary needs affect our mental state, Maslow proposed the idea that we strive to attain a "hierarchy of needs." We acquire elemental requirements hierarchically, ranked based on what is missing in our lives. First, we must assure survival. Once this need is met, we strive for safety, then to fulfill social needs. We seek a sense of belonging and recognition from our peers, followed by an effort to satisfy our need for self-esteem and eventually to find meaning in life. Ideally, as these goals are reached, and one rises through the hierarchy and ultimately realizes one's full potential, one becomes what Maslow called "self-actualized." This attainment envisions a completely developed person who is honest, takes responsibility for its actions, and makes growth decisions instead of decisions based on fear.

Even though you do a variety of things, your life is likely dedicated more to one of the levels of Maslow's Hierarchy Chart, below, than to the other levels.

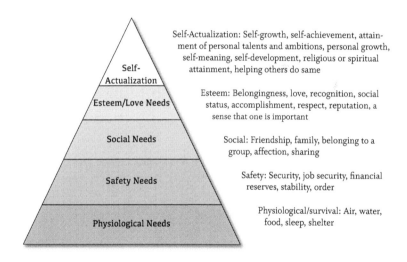

Figure 2.1 Maslow's Hierarchy of Needs Chart[9]

Study the chart above, read the descriptions and ask yourself, "What is my current state of being?"

As you do this, keep in mind, this chart is not meant to imply hierarchy of individual merit. A person should not be categorized, judged, discriminated against, or thought of as being better or worse because of their place on the chart. We all achieve different things at different times.

At the same time though, think of the things you dedicate your life to, in terms of exchanging your life for what you do. Henry David Thoreau said, "The price of anything is the amount of life you exchange for it." Are the things that you are exchanging your life for today truly worth trading your life for? Are these activities truly producing satisfaction that is under your control and will not disappoint?

You might say, "I never think about my life. I just go with the flow." Others might say, "I know what I want and I know where I am going."

This is all well and good, but unless we consciously analyze our lives, it is questionable whether we are really following our will or merely our unconscious impulses. It is important to step back and to view life from a greater perspective.

Our Life's Trajectory

It is important to know where we are in life, how we got here and also where we are going. In some ways, we are like self-directed snowballs, rolling down a hill, stones skipping down the gorge of life. Our thinking and our actions propel our lives forward, like some sort of gravitational pull, but life contains its share of surprises. Our past actions lead to reactions, which causes new actions and reactions and a free-fall that carries us along and changes us.

Søren Kierkegaard mused, "Life must be understood backward, but it must be lived forward."[10] How is this relevant to us? For that matter, how do we understand our lives backward?

Every need has its own strategy for success. We are at every moment either utilizing our best strategy or creating unnecessary difficulty for ourselves. It is therefore important to figure out our desired destination and our current trajectory. Once we know that, we should make every possible effort to reach our ultimate goal. This might require us to educate ourselves in principles of success, to analyze our progress, and to make every effort to walk the path.

Maybe this was one of Kierkegaard's points: We should determine how much our current path in life leads away from the ultimate goal and then see if a course correction is warranted.

The latest findings from neuroscience show that we actually shape and change our brains and nervous systems by the way we think and act. This is good news. It turns out that we are not hard-wired to be who we are. We can change ourselves, our Life's Trajectory, our lives.

Self-directed Neuroplasticity

In a recent article, neuropsychologist Rick Hanson explained,

> All mental activity—sights and sounds, thoughts and feelings, conscious and unconscious processes— is based on underlying neural activity. Day after day, your mind is building your brain. The science of experience-dependent neuroplasticity shows that each one of us has the power to change his or her brain for the better—what Jeffrey Schwartz has called 'self-directed neuroplasticity.[124]

But, according to Hanson, the brain's neuroplasticity also has a dark side.

> If you don't make use of this power yourself, other forces will shape your brain for you, including pressures at work and home, technology and media, pushy people, the lingering effects of painful past experiences, and Mother Nature herself.[124]

Since we tend to self-validate our convictions, beliefs and points of view, it might be possible that our current trajectory in life is contrary to our greatest good. To be sure that we are following our best course of action, it is necessary to examine ourselves, our state of being and our motivations. This requires us to utilize a technique, such as mindfulness meditation, that is greater than mere conscious observation or heartfelt wishful thinking. Above all, we must be honest with ourselves.

Projecting forward, if your life does not change any, how

does it play out? What is your current trajectory? If things keep going the way they are, what will your life be like, what will your state of being be like, in five years, ten, twenty and forty? Just as important, what is your ultimate goal?

The Key to Understanding Happiness

The following quote has been attributed to John Lennon, but it may be apocryphal. Regardless, it makes a great point as to our purpose in life.

> When I was five years old my mother always told me that happiness was the key to life. When I went to school, they asked me what I wanted to be when I grew up. I wrote down 'happy.' They told me I did not understand the assignment, and I told them they did not understand life.

This is poignant. We all have different ideas about what happiness is and how to achieve it, but is not happiness everyone's ultimate goal? Think about the things you enjoy doing; what end-result are they trying to bring about? Is it not a sort of satisfaction the opposite of suffering? Perhaps then, understanding suffering is the key to understanding happiness.

If you were able to observe every second of your existence, unless you have already transcended Self-Actualization, you would probably find that within every second of your being there is some action or thought that tries to avoid stress or suffering on some level. Unless you are able to alleviate your stress internally, you are suffering. You are either working toward some goal that promises to alleviate your suffering, or you are trying to hold on to something that seems to abate suffering.

Even though this process of trying to abate suffering occupies so much of our time and energy, too many do not even take the time to understand what it is that takes so much of their effort.

If you think about the Hierarchy of Needs chart in its initial form, every level has a component that is driven by the desire to avoid stress and suffering and to fulfill ourselves. The important question to ask is, "Which level actually achieves satisfaction or causes the cessation of suffering?"

Once again, what I mean by suffering is that unnecessary psychological stress and inner pain that we feel, that manifests in a number of ways: as outright stress, discontentment, dissatisfaction, frustration, dread, anxiety, depression, boredom, misery and sadness, or any other bad feeling.

Suffering can mean different things to different people on the surface level, but there is a useful way to look at it that is more productive. It is better to say what suffering is *not* and then acknowledge how it manifests in our lives. Suffering is *not* satisfaction, contentment, or equanimity. Suffering might be best described as emotional dissatisfaction with what is occurring in the present moment, because of attachment to an alternate outcome. This produces stress and anxiety. Unnecessary stress is suffering. Therefore, other words for avoidance of suffering, the opposite of suffering, are satisfaction, inner peace, or inner equilibrium.

At first glance, it seems that people suffer due to unwanted circumstances. Life fails to conform to our expectations, and this causes suffering. In reality, suffering is an internal, psychological phenomena that occurs because of the way we perceive reality. Unskilled perception causes us to suffer needlessly and to devote our lives to things that make us busy but unsatisfied.

We feel stress for a variety of legitimate reasons. For example, when we are attacked, feelings of stress are natural and give us the necessary energy to fight or flee, helping us to survive. But once danger has passed, continued stress is unnecessary and detrimental, a form of suffering. Some are mindful of their suffering and work to let it go, while others divert their attention from it until they can no longer do so. Fortunately, there are ways to dissipate suffering. For this, it is important to change one's perceptions at the deepest levels, to understand Life's Conundrum and the limitations of Self-Actualization.

Chapter 4

The Limitations of Self-Actualization

"I am no longer cursed by poverty because
I took possession of my own mind, and that mind
has yielded me every material thing I want, and much
more than I need. But this power of mind is a universal
one, available to the humblest person
as it is to the greatest."
—ANDREW CARNEGIE

L ife presents us with a conundrum, a puzzle that relates to the very essence of why we are alive. We seek survival and also ultimate satisfaction and try to have as much fun as we can, in between, yet the conundrum is that *most activities do not permanently satisfy, even if they feel good* or are beneficial. This is a profound puzzle because if something feels good, one would think it should eventually satisfy us.

Various solutions and partial solutions have been proposed throughout the ages for finding satisfaction, but the answers to this problem are so varied that they cause even more confusion. Some propose that there is no possibility of finding satisfaction, so they ennoble suffering and sometimes even proclaim it good. Others insist that cessation of suffering can only occur after death and that this must be granted to us by God. Some people give up trying to understand the problem or the solution and content themselves with holding on to grand mysteries. Still others say that a solution is obtainable here and now, in this life.

Is Satisfaction Possible?

Neuroscience experiments show that,

> Mindfulness, a psychological process reflecting attention and awareness to what is happening in the present moment, has been associated with increased well-being and decreased depression, and anxiety in both healthy and patient populations. Recent work suggests that mindfulness (and mindfulness training interventions) may foster neuroplastic changes in cortico-limbic circuits responsible for stress and emotion regulation.
>
> Mindful individuals have reduced stress reactivity, and suggest new candidate structural neurobiological pathways linking mindfulness with mental and physical health outcomes.[3]

The reason such studies are significant is that they show that mindfulness decreases suffering—without the practitioner needing to have faith in religious or supernatural concepts, or needing to utilize External Sources of happiness—and these are just the benefits of the psychological act of being mindful. Mindfulness meditation is intensely more powerful. It not only shows the benefits mentioned above but also reduces pain, unpleasantness and pain intensity through multiple brain mechanisms.

For centuries, meditation practitioners have claimed that meditation practice produces inner satisfaction and alleviates suffering. Others argued that such claims were merely subjective speculations based on personal experience, untestable and not grounded in reality. Neuroscience is now confirming what meditation practitioners have been saying all along.

A recent study employing arterial spin labeling (ASL) and functional magnetic resonance imaging found that,

[m]editation reduced all subjects' pain intensity and unpleasantness ratings with decreases ranging from 11 to 70% and from 20 to 93%, respectively. Moreover, meditation-related pain relief was directly related to brain regions associated with the cognitive modulation of pain.

Taken together, these findings indicate that both cortico-cortical and cortico-thalamic interactions provide potential substrates for executive-order processes to alter the elaboration of nociceptive information into a subjectively available pain experience.

One might also argue that meditation's pain-relieving effects are simply due to divided attention rather than any unique attributes of mindfulness meditation per se. We believe, that this explanation is unlikely, as it fails to incorporate the differences in the mental processes involved between the two. Moreover, in studies directly comparing meditation to distraction, meditation reduced pain ratings more than distraction (Sedan et al., 2010b) and activated emotion regulatory brain regions (PFC, ACC) to a greater extent than distraction (Holzel et al., 2007).[126]

So how do mindfulness techniques relate to our ultimate goal and to our everyday struggles of living?

The first few levels of the Hierarchy of Needs are dedicated to the purpose of biological continuation. This is dependent on manipulating the external world. Our bodies are hard-wired to feel good when we survive and survive well. This very mechanism works wonderfully for its purpose. However, after we have achieved a stable means of continued survival, then this natural reward system becomes deceptive, especially when we are trying to achieve higher aims, such as inner fulfillment.

After achieving safety and survival, we then strive to feel good. All the hierarchical needs beyond safety and survival needs relate to our psychological well-being. One would think that feeling good and receiving pleasant sensations from External Sources would then, eventually, lead to permanent satiation. But, as mentioned before, external activities, no matter how good they feel, do not bring lasting satisfaction—and this is the cornerstone of the puzzle that makes the conundrum so difficult for most people to figure out. Not being aware of Life's Conundrum, people continually seek pleasures that lead to disappointment—and here, the pattern, described below, becomes clear:

• Sometimes things that are pleasant are not good for us.

- At other times, what seems boring or dissatisfying produces inner peace.

- Happiness that is reliant on things that may change is likely to produce suffering.

- Our attachment to pleasant but changing things is the very reason why life is too often not to our liking, full of stress, dissatisfaction, disappointment and suffering.

But what is it that does not change? Change is the heart of living. Everything changes, right?

If our internal state of being is our reality, then, even though this technically changes, it does not change for us because we are always us. In other words, *if we are concentrated on and dwelling in the moment, on mindfulness, then we utilize a type of satisfaction that comes from within.*

This is the answer to Life's Conundrum, and for this I should explain the difference between External and Internal Sources of happiness.

External versus Internal Sources

If you quantify the goal that we are all seeking after we attain survival and call it ultimate satisfaction and then compare all the possible ways proposed by thinkers throughout history to attain such a goal, you might find that the answer vacillates between two major groups of possibilities. This is extremely important for you to know. All these different methodologies try to solve Life's Conundrum either through *External or Internal Sources.*

If something ultimately emanates from outside of us, then it should rightfully be considered an external solution to the problem, or an External Source. On the other hand, if the solution is created by us internally, controlled and sustained by our own mind, then the solution is an internal one.

One way to draw a distinction between internal and external is to analyze a source and keep it in mind for comparison. Take texting on your cell phone, for example. If you allow it to, the text can affect your feelings, actions, and plans—and then it disappears again. When you read a text, your responses and feelings are internal, but your reaction is catalyzed by and dependent on an External Source. So the key here is how an External Source affects you from outside.

Too many of us focus on *how* coping feels and strive to reproduce that feeling, but we forget to be aware of *where this inner feeling* comes from, *what* the source of the solution is, *how* it is generated and most importantly, its ultimate psychological cost in relation to benefit.

Why are these things important? The reason this realization is important is that it helps us look at the sources and costs of our satisfaction to determine how taxing and sustainable these sources are to our being. Are we dealing with our stress without harming ourselves and others (this is what I mean by cost)? And is the solution actually working as intended?

Imagine meeting a person who could make you instantly happy. Even though you might feel happiness inside you when you're near them, they could walk back out the door, play games with you, die, or be no longer able to help you. Would they not become an attachment, a chain? For would you not be dependent on something that you have limited control over? You might feel that you are unable to live without them. Being away from them would be misery. If you know someone who makes you feel this way, try asking yourself, "Is this person the source of my happiness?" If so, then this is an externally based solution. Your happiness is being caused by something outside yourself. Do you begin to see that the greater our attachments to external things that are not under our control, the more misery they are able to cause us?

Would it not be better to learn to be centered then to have relationships with people without being dependent on them, just enjoying them for who they are, growing with them and striving toward actualization together?

Now let's compare External to Internal Sources. Let's say you are able to sit down and—without the aid of anything external, including anything supernatural—to meditate and produce a compassionate, loving and peaceful state of mind from which to act and achieve life's bounties. You would then not be dependent on anything outside of your control.

Let us use another example, one that is even more in-depth: consider a book. At first, when you read a book, the pictures you see in your mind's eye, the voice of the author and even the internalized ideas you discover are *experienced within* you, yet the information *emanates from a source external to you*; the book is an External Source. But after you read the book and internalize its message and no longer use the book, then you are using a source that is within; the information that now inspires you *belongs* to you, and the book itself becomes irrelevant. You are now using an Internal Source.

One caveat here, though. American science fiction writer Philip K. Dick said it very well: "Reality is whatever refuses to go away when I stop believing in it."[11] Related to this, there are two extremely important distinctions that need to be made that will help us evaluate Internal Sources—*Internal Sources are not all of equal value.* Some merely lead to Self-Actualization. Some sources, even though they are internal, are based on imagination rather than reality and may ask us to focus and be dependent on external things. Other Internal Sources might be unreal, ridiculous, or unbelievable to you and thus unable to cause cessation of suffering. For example, if someone told you that all you had to do was think about a green jellybean to cease suffering, and that did not work, then this source, even though it is internal, would be of no use to you. Choose only Internal Sources that work, that are natural and do not lead to attachment or delusion.

Critical thinking The mental process of actively and skillfully conceptualizing and analyzing information to reach a conclusion. A purposeful and reflective judgment about what to believe in response to observations, experience, verbal or written expressions, and arguments.

A Vision of Things to Come

I awoke in the middle of the night, as if frozen. I could not move my body. I perceived a vision, as if I was really there and it was truly happening to me. I was old and weak, lying on my deathbed. I was surrounded by all the things I traded my life to accumulate—and everything that was once mine was being given away. My body was dying and I would soon cease to exist. As I reflected on this, I realized that this was not just my future; it was *our* future, your future.

I had just experienced my own metaphorical death. We love, we live, we help others and we trade our lives to accumulate pleasant experiences, activities that feel good and should satisfy us, but they do not. This, my nemesis, Life's Conundrum, puzzled me for a long time, but this night terror motivated me to look at my life and helped me realize that Externals would never bring me lasting peace.

There seems to be a usual rite of passage in the West, and my life was following this pattern. We go through stages: childhood, school, partying, an attempt to attain financial success, getting married, having children. Then, life becomes less spontaneous, governed by responsibilities. This often leads to states of being that seem empty and unfulfilling. Eventually, our final days ensue, we scramble, but then it's too late. I wondered, *Perhaps I could live it differently...?*

At first, I really thought that the more I indulged and "lived," the better off I would be, so I pursued pleasure wholeheartedly. I drank, experimented with recreational drugs, socialized and partied as much as possible to achieve satisfaction. I had fun. I experienced extremely good times—and even made lifelong friends. However, these things did not satisfy. Eventually, I realized that pleasure failed to bring me peace.

Partying, even when it was over the top and intense, was unsatisfying in the end. Intense experiences made me crave even more intense experiences, so it made everyday life seem drab and boring. I became jaded and hardened. I realized that partying was an externally based diversion, and that dedicating life to pleasure would only make me want more. It would not yield ultimate satisfaction. So after having my fill of partying, I turned to attainment of financial success.

Does it not seem sometimes that the world is powered by the conviction that financial success is the ultimate satisfaction maker? At one time, I truly believed that wealth was the key factor to achieving all our hierarchical needs. By this time my Physiological, Safety, Social and Esteem Needs were met. I resolved to start a business, fulfill my potential, utilize my talents and attain Self-Actualization, along with the other goals and objects I desired. As soon I set my mind to achieve financial success, I met Dan.

Dan was the owner of a company I worked for, where I learned running a successful business required a no-nonsense, success-oriented approach. He was extremely intelligent and insightful. He explained the "why" behind things. We often had philosophical discussions, and analyzed situations and possibilities. This helped me understand how things functioned and why people did what they did, and it helped me understand a bit more about my own motivations.

When I look back at my life before I met Dan, it seems I was living in a haze. At that time, my life was concentrated on everything but Self-Actualization. Dan had logical answers for most things, a clear way of looking at situations, of taking into account desired results and understanding how to reverse-engineer a process to achieve desired goals.

I soon saw that, basically, every situation had an optimal answer. The key was to hypothesize the likeliest outcomes, test your conclusions and keep on the course until you achieved success. One should not expect that things would just happen. Luck was not enough and fate was just an illusion. One needed to delay instant gratification and make things happen. Reality had to be observed, meaning obtained and synthesized, and the shortest and most effective path to the goal determined.

I marveled that there were such clear-cut explanations and that they made sense. The everyday world no longer appeared puzzling. I felt I understood why people did what they did and why things functioned the way they did. Everything could be understood if one took enough time to analyze and study it.

I know now that Dan was exercising critical thinking skills and teaching me how to make decisions based on logic, reason and positive thinking. It is too easy to feel an emotion and go with it without first using the intellect. If we do this with important decisions, things can go badly, without our even realizing it. At the same time, there are people who need to get in touch with their feelings because they are repressing them. Perhaps it is best to have a balance. Critical thinking helped me to find this equilibrium.

Most importantly, Dan introduced me to the power of the unconscious mind. When critical thinking is combined with information gathered from the subconscious, it becomes a powerful catalyst on the path of actualization. It allows deep-seated knowledge to be combined with logic and reason, enhancing information gathered and helping one to determine the best course of action.

Dan introduced me to positive thinking and neuro-linguistic programming (NLP). He recommended books and showed me that these things worked. At the time, some of my favorites were *Think and Grow Rich*, by Napoleon Hill, *Psycho Cybernetics*, by Maxwell Maltz, *The Richest Man in Babylon* by George S. Clayson and *Unlimited Power* by Anthony Robbins.

These books empowered me. My imagination was the only limit. When I became convinced that I could achieve anything I wanted, I determined my goals and set my auto-pilot, the unconscious mind, to have it achieve my desires. I realized that nothing was beyond my abilities if I wanted it badly enough.

Within months I started my own company, and as I began to grow my business, I experienced more of the finer things in life. Positive thinking worked. However, as I attained my goals, my life became repetitive. This was much better than being stuck in some life pattern that was unsuccessful and negative, but my desires were insatiable. As soon as I achieved a goal, another goal took its place and I still felt empty inside.

Learning and then expressing competency are aspects of normal growth. So I will agree that expressions of craftsmanship, of helping others and of hard work can exhibit powerful levels of creativity and self-growth, providing deep satisfaction and a period of fulfillment. But even the utmost skill and "genius-level" work falls short of permanent satisfaction. It fills a block of time, but it does not offer an internal source of peace. Once you have achieved one goal, you are bound to seek another. The danger is that we become expert at filling minutes without increasing our inner satisfaction. Like a hungry ghost, the empty self cannot be filled with whatever activities fill our time.

I know, a jeweler is not necessarily disappointed between creating rings, yet that itch does not go away and its cycle continues. Perhaps there is something to that old saying, "The more we achieve, the more we want." This reminds me of what Henry David Thoreau noticed: "Men have become the tools of their tools."[12]

Or you might remember the mythical story of Sisyphus. Sisyphus was an ancient Greek king who was punished by the gods and forced to roll a large boulder up a hill, only to watch it roll back, cursed to constantly repeat this for all eternity.[13] The word *sisyphean* means endless and unavailing in achieving a goal.

Think of that successful business executive or any person who does not practice his or her business with inner peace and inner independence and is enslaved by cycles of failure and success. Her life is shallower than it appears to be on the outside, being all-goal, lose-or-win, self-centered, ego-driven and concentrated on the empty self. Is she not a modern-day Sisyphus doomed to perpetuate her endless ritual, pushing that giant boulder all day, only to have to start again in the morning? Is she not enslaved by his version of golden chains, linked to tasks that fail to satisfy? There is no inner peace on top of that hill! If she stops, the path is still there waiting, but if she continues, she gets nowhere!

Almost every modern way of coping with day-to-day life is predicated on a faulty understanding of what will satisfy us.

Let us compare a career to a fishing rod, hunting bow or spear. In "native environments," or in ancient times, these simple tools provided the same things that your career gives you now a living, a means of providing safety and security, a way of using your talents. A career is something more than a simple job; it is perhaps a way to fulfill a lifestyle, to attain Social and Esteem Needs, to use talents and help humanity. Maybe, it is even a way to reach Self-Actualization. One's career may lead to economic security and freedom, which are important in satisfying our basic hierarchical needs, but is a career an Internal or an External Source? Does it change? Is it under our control?

Financial success was beneficial. It felt good, it diverted my attention away from my immediate suffering, it allowed me the ability to express my loves and talents, it offered me a great lifestyle and permitted me to help others, but it did not give me the ultimate satisfaction that I needed. It turned out to be a roller coaster of unending craving and attainment. Financial success should be achieved for its own sake, not for the hope that it will bring inner peace. However, since that familiar inner emptiness returned, I needed a new way to try to find satisfaction.

I became convinced that inter-personal relationships would make me satisfied. I dreamed of finding my soul mate, my life-long best friend. We would be truly in love, share an understanding, deep feelings, a bond and admiration for one another. It is true that romantic relationships are fertile soil for self-actualized growth. Two people can become a "mirror" for one another; they can share insights and become transformed, give and learn, perhaps even ascend the Hierarchy of Needs together.

However, as I began to experience deep relationships, as beautiful as they were, I realized that relationships required maturity, time, work, commitment and communication. Relationships were hardly the easy, problem-free, live-for-ever-after affairs we see in movies. Love and beauty can be misleading; it can distract us from the suffering that lies within us for a time, but when that honeymoon phase ends and the romance no longer serves as a distraction, we once again notice life's suffering. Rather than realizing that love is not meant to make us happy and working on inner peace, we often find ourselves looking for the next fix, blaming past relationships and finding fault with the other person, rather than dealing with our own inner pain.

Perhaps what we get out of relationships sometimes is a surprise, a "wake up call." The emotional depth involved in getting close requires great psychological investment and leaves people vulnerable to one another. Intimacy touches our emotional core and sometimes even aggravates deep-seated issues.

Romantic love brings pleasure and satisfies our Social and Esteem Needs, but it cannot fill our psychic wounds, nor should it be counted on to *center* our being. I've been married for more than a decade; my wife and I have a soul mate relationship that is extremely fulfilling. But we both recognize the importance of inner work. This makes our relationship even better: is it not better to enjoy other people, love them, be with them and also enhance the relationship by having an equanimity that comes from within, that is not needy or dependent on someone else, on External Sources?

Eventually, even the deepest infatuations and soulmate relationships end; love, too, stakes all its hopes and dreams on a person who is mortal and transient, who has free will, and separations can be devastating. Maybe it is for these reasons that people who stake their inner peace on love often wind up disenchanted and hurt.

It is necessary to make an important point here: many reading this would wish with all their hearts to achieve a relationship that you or I would describe as being with a soul mate. But this is also the core truth inside my point. Do find your soul mate! Cherish them and travel the path with them if you need this, by all means, but know that you *must work on your own inner peace as well.* You will still need to address the inner hurt that is responsible for your current state of being. Love will not dispel your depression and nightmares for long. *Acquire that inner-centeredness.*

I suppose that family life carries the same longings and expectations as love. Depending on how we internalize our roles and expectations, it too can be an External Source of happiness. What does the concept of having a family really mean to us? Anyone who has raised children knows there are hundreds of magic moments that only happen between a parent and a child and that for most people, being a parent is a remarkable joy. Even so, it should not be done with the expectation that it will lead to ultimate happiness.

Young parents often have an idealized dream of creating the perfect family, of continuously sharing love and of having it returned, of children who are the best, the smartest and the most successful and of this situation providing ultimate happiness. However, eventually our ideas of parenthood probably become more realistic.

Parents who toil endlessly to provide for their families and who sacrifice their greater good for the people who count on them often do so out of love without expecting the same considerations or even some ultimate happiness at the end of all their work. A loving parent accepts and loves their child even though they might not turn out to be the best, smartest, healthiest, the most successful, or the most loving. Our children might suffer adversity, just like everyone else, no matter how much we try to help them, and eventually, whether things work out well for our children or not, they will leave us to pursue their own paths, so family life cannot even guarantee happiness for parents during their older years.

As much as it is a shared life with people who are often closer to us than anyone else, family life is a full-time occupation. Realistically, it might offer as much struggle as it does those happy moments. It is a worthwhile path, full of lessons, but if history has anything to say about hopes, dreams and family, it might show us that family life cannot be relied on to provide inner peace.

It dawned on me as I reflected on these things that family life, too, should be done for its own sake, for the inherent goodness of sharing life and love with others, but it is not wise of anyone to expect ultimate satisfaction from it.

During my search to figure out Life's Conundrum, a friend offered me something that made me think. She invited me to her church. *Was this perhaps the way to lead the ideal life and to gain that internal happiness?* I wondered.

But upon further reflection, I realized that so many of the people I knew who practiced religious beliefs were still not freed from their stress and suffering. I too had experienced this when I was a child; I practiced my religion with my whole heart and full faith. Christianity provided emotional comfort at times but not ongoing solace that was derived from Internal Sources. Besides, theistic religion required belief in concepts that I was not sure were true.

When I returned to religion as an adult, I received similar results. I worshipped and opened up my heart to the love of Jesus, and this was fulfilling to an extent, but it was not the type of inner peace that I experienced later when meditating and working with the unconscious mind. I even tried practicing different religions, with the same result.

Perhaps this should not have surprised me. Theistic religion asks us to depend on God, a source outside ourselves, that we have little or no control over, that may not even exist, and thus its practices are in the realm of Self-Actualization.

Stuck?

As I reflected on the hierarchical chart—my place on it and on my ultimate goal—I had the earth-shattering suspicion that by following Self-Actualization, I could never truly go beyond the emptiness that I felt inside, beyond my "empty self"—"self" being used as another word for conditioned personality, an illusion. Self-Actualization, the way it was practiced by most people, concentrated on catering to the empty self, to the personality, to bolstering it rather than moving beyond it.

Therefore, all the levels up to and including Self-Actualization concentrated on external actualizations, and this is why even Self-Actualization leaves us dissatisfied.

The Self-Actualized people I was familiar with had fun in life, financial success, loving relationships and nurturing family lives; they were sometimes religious and active members of their community, but they were still not satisfied and suffered internally. Self-Actualization made many of them masters at chasing objects and goals, catching and achieving them, but often the satisfaction earned from attaining external goals and dreams tended to fade and disappear, leaving them continually yearning to take up the chase again, like golden chains that bind us to a pattern of living only attached to fleeting objects, one that is never satisfied.

As I studied further, I grew convinced that Self-actualization did not fully satisfy. How would I move forward and attain ultimate satisfaction? What good was it to know one's predicament if one is not able to change the circumstances? I felt more confused than ever because at the time I knew nothing about Inner-Actualization.

I decided to apply critical thinking to the problem. I went to the library and to bookstores to do more research. I brought home stacks of books to read. I wanted to find out how wise people throughout the centuries had solved this puzzle and had eradicated their own innate suffering and found ultimate satisfaction.

I started with those sources that were the oldest, that had asked these questions thousands of years ago. I needed to read books that were considered so important and fundamental that they changed civilizations. I read the Bible and the Koran, the Torah and its commentaries, the Hindu Bhagavad Gita, the Rigveda and the Upanishads, Gnostic texts, Jain and Zoroastrian works and my favorite Buddhist works, such as the Tripitaka. I also looked into Western

philosophy and even read books by Eastern European writ-
ers such as Fyodor Dostoyevsky and Leo Tolstoy, especially
concentrating on their philosophical works. I counter-bal-
anced all that with reading about how science perceived the
workings of the mind. I read books on philosophy, psychology and psychotherapy and those that contained Atheistic,
secular and hedonistic messages. I wanted to get opposing views. I didn't care if the path I found was religious or
secular, as long as it was the truth and I could believe and
practice it. I contemplated the nature of life, trying to find
a common denominator between all the different possibilities. Then I realized something meaningful: Self-Actualization contained a serious limitation. This was a conundrum.

The realizations that I raise here are difficult to come
to terms with. In these last few paragraphs, I have outlined
why living a pleasant life, doing things that matter, loving
and experiencing pleasure is not enough to attain inner
peace. This probably goes against everything you have ever
heard or read.

My career, attainments and diversions, inter-personal
relationships and religion left me wanting more. I still suffered and remained unfulfilled, even though my activities
should have satisfied me. Up to that point in my life, I had
achieved my Physiological, Safety, Social, Esteem and Self-
Actualization Needs, but this did not eradicate the empty
sense of self that I felt.

My Life's Trajectory, my "current state of being," was
dissatisfaction. If I kept leading the same lifestyle, I would
be no better off tomorrow than I was today. So I wondered:
What is the solution to this problem? What is the ideal life? I felt

stuck. I did not know the answer until I re-examined the Hierarchy of Needs. I then realized what was missing.

Chapter 5

Inner-Actualization

Inner-Actualization versus Self-Actualization

In the last half of the nineteenth and early twentieth century, neurologist and psychotherapist Sigmund Freud developed a psychodynamic model of mental health that viewed the unconscious mind as home to primitive instincts and sometimes evil intent and the conscious mind as being where the ego is involved in our actions and impulses, where we process our emotions, thoughts and fears.[14]

Because so much of this psychodynamic methodology dealt with unhealthy people, a new wave of practitioners that included Rogers and Maslow gained prominence in the second half of the twentieth century. Their brand of psychology arrived at its insights by studying healthy, flourishing subjects and postulating ways to achieve a more positive, integrated personality.

Unfortunately, Maslow and his colleagues viewed well-being as a hierarchical pyramid and assumed that along with personal achievements one would also attain satisfaction and inner peace. He and his followers also failed to make a distinction between Internal and External Sources of happiness. If our personal growth path is too focused on challenges outside ourselves, then our lives will most likely lack the focus necessary to develop *inner independence*.

As we view Life's Conundrum, the observation that pleasant things and current successes do not always satisfy, it becomes evident that Maslow's definition of Self-Actualization does not take into account the difference between Internal and External sources.[9] This casts too wide a net. This definition is problematic because it uses two opposing methodologies in a single concept and contains the possibility for someone to try to pursue ultimate satisfaction through Self-Actualization by being dependent on external factors that change and disappoint, and thus this concept requires that careful distinctions be made.

To help this, I highlighted this distinction and created a new definition for Self-Actualization: satisfaction that is primarily based on External Sources. Inner-Actualization, on the other hand, is a psychological state of being based on Internal Sources that produce inner peace, an ultimate state of satisfaction combined with a general lack of the debilitating psychological stress that leads to suffering. Figure 5.1 (below) shows how Inner-Actualization solves the problem of Life's Conundrum and moves us beyond Self-Actualization; it empowers free will and leads to the fulfillment of personal growth and meaning without hierarchical considerations.

Figure 5.1 Inner-Actualized Needs Chart

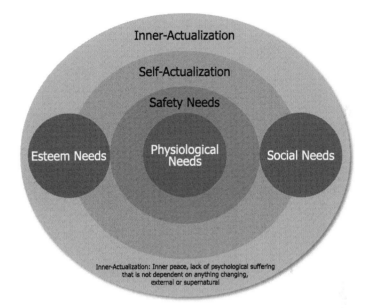

Your Inner-Actualization

Your life is now concentrated on one of these levels more than on the others. In essence, we are all trying to survive or derive our life's utmost satisfaction from these sources.

Other than safety and survival, these levels are different ways to achieve ultimate satisfaction. Yet none of them satisfies until we are in charge of our own psychological state of being in such a way that we are not dependent on the changing nature of life. But reading about this or knowing it intellectually without *doing* is merely the first step. What then should we do?

The questions to ask yourself are: *Where does my satisfaction come from? How do I obtain my meaning in life? Are these internal or external, am I aiming for Self-Actualization or Inner-Actualization?*

This is a simple but significant insight: if you still get attached to things, be aware of your attachments and work on becoming inwardly centered instead of needing so many external props.

Attachments are to be expected within the psychological practices of Self-Actualization, while Inner-Actualization concentrates on using our internal states of being to produce inner independence. Therefore, above all, determine whether your sources of actualization emanate from Internal or External Sources.

Needs versus Wants A "need" is anything that is essential for life or health. A "want" is anything that is not essential for life or health. Anything that is not a need is a want. Wants are usually insatiable, diversions from our suffering.

Inner-Actualized Needs:

1. **Physiological Needs**: Survival, air, water, food, and sleep
2. **Safety Needs**: Protection, job security, financial reserves, stability, limits
3. **Social/Love Needs**: Friendship, family, belonging, affection and sharing
4. **Esteem Needs**: Recognition, social status, accomplishment, respect and reputation, feeling valuable
5. **Self-Actualization**: Achievement, fulfillment of personal talents and ambitions, personal growth and development, sense of meaning...
6. **Inner-Actualization:** Mindfulness, inner satisfaction, inner peace not dependent on externals...

Internal Sources Anything that is under our control and not transient, causes cessation of suffering and originally emanates from our mind.

External Sources Anything that emanates from outside of us, often produces temporary cessation of suffering and dependence; an attachment or golden chain.

Inner-Actualization A state of inner peace and satisfaction that continues regardless of the circumstances, based on Internal Sources that are not dependent on anything supernatural, resulting in a centered understanding of life's ultimate meaning; a state of mind free from psychological suffering. Inner-Actualization uses Internal Sources and mindfulness to clear the unconscious mind of encumbrances to cease the hindrances that cause suffering.

Chapter 6

A New Way of Looking Inward?

*"The people have a right to truth, as they have a right
to life, liberty and the pursuit of happiness."*
—EPICTETUS

As neuroscience makes unparalleled advances in mapping the structure and function of the nervous system and the brain, psychology and hypnotherapy continue to advance, and ancient meditation techniques keep using time-tested methods to harness the power of the mind. It is time now to unite these various technologies and bring forth a greater awareness without using archaic language and traditions that are unnecessary remnants of ancient foreign cultures. The concept of Inner-Actualization is not new. It is a recognition that our state of mind has everything to do with the condition of our lives and that we are in charge of it, even though the untamed mind wreaks havoc and makes excuses for why it suffers.

In the past, "Mental processes and disorders were [usually explained as being]…magical actions caused by external forces."[15] For example, when a person felt miserable, did something regrettable, or was ill, explanations often relied on mythology, demonology and animism.[16] *Masters of the Mind* is a book that explores the history of mental health and explains how "Magic and supernatural concepts helped early humans to make sense out of the many unfathomable and unpredictable aspects of prehistoric life."[15] The reason this is important to consider is that magical explanations fail to empower the individual and instead give that power to some External Source. Each of us has the ability to create a wonderful inner sense of being. Therefore, from here forward, we will call any explanation that relies on blind faith "magical thinking."

Starting in at least the sixth century BCE, an alternative to magical thinking arose. Some "philosophers and scientists began to speculate intelligently about a wide range of psychological processes."[15] They explained existence through natural occurrences. The core foundations of their philosophy celebrated critical thinking and scientific inquiry. People such as Hippocrates and Galen "attributed actions, thoughts and feelings to natural forces, that is, to forces within themselves…Many of their ideas turned out to be remarkably far sighted."[15] A specific example from ancient Greece, in his book about epilepsy and mental illness, Hippocrates says,

> Those who first connected this illness [epilepsy] with demons and described it as sacred seem to me no different than the conjurers, purificators, mountebanks and charlatans of our day. Such persons are

merely concealing, under the cloak of godliness, their perplexity and their inability to afford any assistance... It's not a god that injures the body, but a disease.[15]

Hundreds of years later, an ancient pre-Christian Roman says,

The more cultured classes of Rome were determined to eliminate magic and superstition in considering psychic processes.... Transcendental mythologies were regarded as superstitious beliefs that originated from fear and ignorance.[15]

We certainly know that some ancients were prone to magical thinking and to worshipping strange gods. But clearly, reason, critical thinking and creativity were valued in ancient Greece and Rome. Even though there was a rivalry between magical and critical thinkers, these two ways of looking at the world lived side-by-side in the pagan ancient world for centuries. The very nature of polytheism allows different sects and philosophies to exist together, as long as they are not in direct competition militarily. Maybe it was this spirit of tolerance that led to technological advancements and the Golden Ages of Greece and Rome? After all, it was innovation and superior technology that gave the pre-Christian Greco-Roman world its edge over Christian Rome, whether that edge was military, philosophical, architectural or artistic.

However, after the Western Roman Empire was overrun by its enemies, rather than being resuscitated to its former glory with innovation, Rome slid into irreversible decline.

The Eastern half, the Byzantine Empire, continued to exist for almost a thousand years, until about 1461.[17] But it too was unable to surpass, or even re-create the intellectual and economic growth and prosperity of the pagan Roman period. Even though "[i]ts central geographic position ... spices and other exports virtually guaranteed wealth and stability,"[18] its biggest achievement is, arguably, the preservation of pagan advancements. Scholars fleeing Byzantium in roughly the 10th through the 13th centuries helped reintroduce the works they took with them to the West. Some have argued that repatriation of these previously lost texts to the West helped to spark the Renaissance.[19] What does this have to do with Inner-Actualization?

For a time, science, critical thinking and even meditation of the type that works to achieve Inner-Actualization surfaced in ancient, pre-Christian Rome. Had it continued, there is a good chance that the culture of inner peace would have been a long-held Western tradition. But pagan Rome fell, replaced by an authoritarian Christian church that was sometimes intolerant of competing philosophies. The Christian version of magical thinking held that unhappiness and disease were caused by supernatural forces seeking to harm humanity. This did little to empower the common person to transcend the unstilled mind.[20]

Where did the church's magical thinking come from? It drew on a theological tradition that dated back to an age when magic was accepted as being real. While Christianity's direct ancestor is Judaism, some of its foundations lie in other, earlier Middle Eastern civilizations. Ancient Persian mythology leaves a remarkable legacy that affects some us even today.[21]

The Persian empire was established about 900 BCE and flourished until about 300 BCE...The Persians considered all physical disease and mental disorders to be the work of the devil. Moreover, they felt that treatment should be based on a supernatural point of view that employed incantations and exorcism, as well as magical and religious rites. To them, humans were creatures in which the forces of good and evil were struggling for the future of mankind. The rigid religious system and illiteracy of the common person limited reflective growth in both Persia's philosophy and science.[15]

You might ask, "Were not ancient Europeans also superstitious and inclined to magical thinking?" As stated earlier, the pagan world allowed magical and critical thinking to co-exist. One never completely overcame the other. As the Roman Empire declined, magical thinking became dominant because church law became the law of the land. Any philosophy that openly contradicted the church's dogma was eradicated or forced underground.

Was the decline of the Roman Empire really so bad? Some claim that it had little negative effect on the West or that it actually benefited Europe.[22] The facts seem to tell a different story. During this time, Europe gained zero economic growth, life span and per capita income decreased, while infant mortality rose.[23] "[u]ntil beyond the thirteenth century—for nearly a thousand years—there is no advance in medical science on record in Western Europe."[24] It was, for the most part, a place steeped in ancient beliefs, superstition, dogma and magical thinking.[24] Some innovation occurred in other areas, but they paled in comparison with the advances made in previous and subsequent periods.

Obviously, religion does not need to be authoritarian and intolerant. The church should not be blamed for bringing the Roman Empire to ruin and it deserves credit for its positive contributions. But an authoritarian religion had complete control over and ran the political, religious, economic and cultural systems of the empire during its decline. There are facts that show that church leaders discouraged rational inquiry, experimentation, innovation and scientific advancements whenever possible, whenever these would threaten religious dogma and the church's control.[19] If the church ruled inflexibly and intolerantly enough to make magical thinking prevail, stifling freethinking, this could account for further decline. Creativity and innovation were likely the very ingredient needed to save Rome.

Perhaps we will never know exactly why the Dark Ages occurred, or why the Roman Empire fell, but we do know that until the darkness ended in Europe, "the scientific method of the Greeks—observe, hypothesize, test—fell into disuse."[25] The reason critical thinking and the use of reason are important to our quest is because the workings of the mind are not supernatural processes; understanding the mind in a secular way empowers us to achieve inner peace.

The Age of Reason

Reason and innovation gives us the ability to study the nature of the mind. "In 1567, Paracelsus is credited with providing the first scientific mention . . . of the unconscious aspect of cognition."[26] Starting from the seventeenth century, advancements continued. This was significant. Science gained ground and magical cures became less common. The word "unconscious" was coined in the eighteenth century by Friedrich Wilhelm J. Schelling and essayist Samuel Taylor Coleridge.[27] "Wilhelm Wundt and William James defined psychology as the science of mental life and provided insightful discussions of topics and challenges for a science of psychology that anticipated much of the field's research agenda a century later."[20]

People such as Freud, Jung and Erickson took the torch and carried it to the next marker. Subliminally, they started to prove a core point and made it famous even among lay people. The point was that the mind was responsible for how we perceived reality and the self. The mind determined our state of being, and thus, the unconscious mind was the key to human salvation!

What this meant was that mental health, happiness and inner growth could be achieved by accessing the unconscious mind and by changing its unproductive mental patterns without the need of magic, religion, or superstition. To those who understood the implications, this seemed like a revelation of biblical proportions, especially since for many, this nullified, in many ways, much of the superstitious mumbo jumbo that had been foisted on the public over the centuries. This also laid the groundwork for understanding secular spirituality.

Sigmund Freud established psychoanalysis in a Europe cloaked by religious ideas about individual sin at the same time that monolithic political movements made understanding the "archaic vestiges" of man's unconscious forces of paramount importance.[28]

Carl Jung, Freud's contemporary, also believed that psychoanalysis could reveal the heretofore unseen and unknown realm below our conscious mind and make people better. But his understanding of the unconscious was less concerned with sexual neurosis and aggression and more focused on seeing the entire canvas of the human condition, how the archetypes of the collective unconscious guide and support our ability to tame and transcend our instincts.[29] According to Anthony Storr, Jung seemed to be saying that "By paying attention to the voice within, the individual achieves a new synthesis, a sense of calm acceptance and detachment, and a realization of the meaning of life."[30]

While Freud and Jung guided and observed their subjects in trance states and then mapped, analyzed and described these forays into the mind, Milton Erickson founded the American Society for Clinical Hypnosis. He was a psychiatrist, lecturer, author and subject of many books. Specializing in family therapy, he helped inspire several different forms of therapy and revolutionized the field through his pioneering work in medical hypnosis. He is "credited with bringing the techniques of hypnotherapy into mainstream medical and psychological practice and developing its most comprehensive form."[31]

Why is hypnosis relevant to our discussion, and how is it related to the other methods mentioned? In the West, in modern times, hypnosis was *the* original tool used to access the unconscious mind. Since then, it "has been officially endorsed as a therapeutic method by medical, psychiatric, dental, and psychological associations throughout the world."[32]

Over the years, these and various other pioneering

efforts continue to confirm that mental health belongs to the realm of science and medicine, that the unconscious mind affects our deepest urges and behaviors and can be healed and helped. However, the historical account presented above fails to take into account one important factor: the discoveries made in other parts of the world. Therefore, it is sometimes surprising to learn that ancient people in other parts of the world came to similar conclusions as scientists in the West. The outlook that *being* is a psychological state of mind, that mental illness is a natural aberration, and that access to the mind can lead to internal growth and happiness *without* the help of magic and supernatural beings is a secular outlook; but this viewpoint has also been known in the East for thousands of years. This secular, non-supernatural way of viewing spirituality is not exclusively a Western idea!

The Eastern Connection

Critics sometimes argue that science alone is cold, that reason is shallow and that the prodigies of the Age of Enlightenment celebrate materialism bereft of soul and spirituality. They fear that reason threatens to hurtle humanity into irreconcilable error.

Traditional Eastern methods seek to alleviate this concern by giving the intellect access to the depth and wisdom of the unconscious mind. This works to supplement some of the gaps left by using only conscious awareness.

If we were to personify the East and the West, traditionally, the West might be pictured as a scientist standing in a white lab coat, peering through a window into a room where a great experiment is taking place. The scientist collects data, takes notes, measures, quantifies and documents the information. The scientist never steps inside the room and is not subjected to the experiment. She stands apart and uses the knowledge gained for practical purposes rationally, thereby making the world a better place. To some, this might seem too cold and scientific.

Meanwhile, the East might be pictured as the person inside the room, conducting the experiment on himself, affecting change within, meditating, delving into the depths of the unconscious mind, becoming transformed and serving as an example to others. Then, afterwards, if this is helpful or warranted, the meditator inside the room takes note of what occurred, explains and documents the experiment, thereby transforming himself and the world through personal action.

The Eastern method delves into the depths and produces insights. The Western method tests and confirms the facts. Alone they are sometimes incomplete; together they touch and heal the human spirit. The blending of Eastern and Western mastery coalesces into a unified whole. I am not blind to the shortcomings of either East or West, but it is time now to benefit from the experience of both approaches. When we combine the knowledge that humanity has discovered in the last two thousand years, what we find is that Western science and psychology confirms many of the deep spiritual experiences actualized in the East.

The Seeming Differences Between East and West

The East has its own pioneers who explored the far reaches of mind and mental health. Since the list is long, I will mention three. The last two created systems that are fully functional in modern times.

In ancient China, people such as Hsun Tzu, 298–212 BCE, argued that "rational thought and empirical procedures were more significant than superstitious beliefs."[15] The Yellow Emperor's Inner Canon, or *Neijing Suwen,* was written circa 475–221 BCE and discusses mental illnesses such as amnesia and epilepsy without attributing their cause to supernatural entities.[33] Written in India, circa 586–483 BCE, the Theravada Pali Canon, otherwise known as the Tipitaka,[34] shows how to use meditation to access the unconscious mind and to alleviate mental suffering without need of or help from gods or spirits.[35] The Tipitaka is attributed to Siddhartha Gautama the Buddha.[36]

Before I tried mindfulness meditation, I expected Buddhist meditation techniques to be based on supernatural formulas, on worshipping the Buddha and on faith in foreign gods. My assumptions were incorrect. Mindfulness is secular enough not to offend even the most ardent of Atheists, such as neuroscientist Sam Harris, who is often referred to as one of the "Four Horsemen" along with Richard Dawkins, Christopher Hitchens and Daniel Dennett. But Harris is a proponent of mindfulness meditation.

This technique is historically successful. It has helped millions of people since the fifth century BCE. Neuroscience is now studying its effectiveness. It is proving to increase compassion and well-being and to decrease stress, suffering, depression and anxiety.[126]

Thus, mindfulness meditation, because it is neutral and it works, serves as the perfect mechanism for working on Inner-Actualization.

What about the Buddha's overall teachings? Admittedly, I sometimes find old translations of the Tipitaka stuffy. Most versions are written in an arcane language by ancient people who were not exposed to the latest discoveries of the twenty-first century, and some parts do sound mystical.

However, the core idea held by the Buddha, that of enlightenment, is revolutionary in that it is not based on supernaturalism, but on psychology. According to the Tipitaka, the Buddha did not intend for people to worship him or any deity. In fact, he warned against the pitfalls of worship, calling people to do their own work.[37] He did not even name the people who followed his teachings "Buddhists." This was a later invention. The cornerstone of Gautama's methods was his meditation techniques, and they did not rely on magic, supernatural antidotes, theism or even on conversion to Buddhism.[39]

In the last 2,500 years, the Buddha's teaching has circled the globe, has been reinterpreted by successive generations and has evolved into different versions in order to remain relevant to the cultures in which it exists. Even though some traditional forms of Buddhism choose to believe in supernatural things, arguably, the cornerstone of Buddhism is its teaching of right conduct, wisdom and meditation (*sila, samadhi, panna*). It is important to note that a new interpretation of Buddhism is forming, and it centers on these three fundamental elements. It is sometimes referred to as Secular Buddhism.

Secular Buddhism makes no supernatural claims and advocates only those elements that are consistent with or corroborated by reason and the best science available. Its beliefs are held only on facts, while any other information is considered opinion or hypothesis. I think this aims at the root of what the Buddha taught.

He did not use the words conscious and unconscious mind; these are 18th century coinages,[27] but it is plain to see that the Buddha understood the mind, seeing it as the root and the solution to our problems. Even though his teachings were sometimes misunderstood, his prescriptions were psychological. He asked us to access the unconscious mind to change the programming that limited us. His primary aim was to free people from suffering,[40] and this is identical with the aims of Inner-Actualization. The Buddha not only identified the problem philosophically; he also tested his hypotheses on himself before he taught the masses. It is said that through these methods, he achieved the ultimate goal. If this is true, he was *one of* the first Inner-Actualizers, But according to him, not *the* first. Nor will he be the last. Anyone can achieve a heightened state of being. He specifically warns us that the other alternative, indulgence in external and transient distractions, seems like true happiness, seeming to free us from suffering, but this is an illusion. Transient things work initially but cause attachment to things that are beyond our control.[40] He called this "becoming,"[41] and he referred to the ability of "reflection on the inadequacy and limitation of the conditioned world" as *Adinavakatha*, which is coupled with and exasperated by the elements of *anicca*, meaning impermanent/impermanence, *dukkha*, meaning suffering and *anattā*, or not-self.[40]

If one looks at Gautama's work in its proper relation to his stated goals, it is clear that his is a secular and pragmatic methodology.[42] He taught that inner peace was attained through mindfulness of those elements that produced a centered state of being, that accessing the unconscious through meditation was essential and that this eradicates our innate human suffering.[43] He reminds us that our actions, mental and physical, produce reactions.

The Buddha called this *karma*, or *kamma*, a word that has been greatly misperceived over the ages. Some understand the term in a way that is exactly opposite to how it was meant. They say things like, "It's my *karma*; I'm doomed." These words should not contain any sort of supernatural meaning. Our psychological reactions form our "trajectory," our "current state of being"—they are our karma. Likewise, mental practices that change the negative processes of the unconscious mind allow us to feel better and make a better life for ourselves, despite our current mental trajectory. We change our karma by changing our current mental state of being.[43]

Amazingly, twenty-five hundred years later, Freud, Jung and Erickson came to some of the same core conclusions as the Buddha. While there are significant differences between their systems, they all agreed with the assessment that mental health can be achieved by accessing the unconscious mind. Practitioners of early Buddhism define enlightenment as having seven factors that produce a state of being free from suffering.[169] Whether we call these factors happiness, nirvana or something else altogether, these individuals do seem to agree that changing unproductive mental patterns eradicates suffering and leads to happiness.

To some, this is a radical charge. Some still credit internal change to supernatural factors, believing that enlightenment and ultimate happiness are mystical manifestations, not psychological ones, and can only be granted by the grace of God(s), divine spirits or supernatural forces. They think blessings and curses are caused by faith or lack thereof, by religious acts, rites and rituals. Maybe this is why some still view the psyche with suspicion, fear and wonder.

Some might object to putting the Buddha in the same category as Freud, Jung and Erickson; they might see this as being blasphemous, or an attempt to elevate "mere scientists" to "Buddha status." Others might see this as some sort of misguided attempt to legitimize Eastern mysticism. But to truly understand the core of the matter, it is important to know that altered states of consciousness are not mystical occurrences.[44] While it could be argued that the Buddha used meditation to achieve enlightenment and the others did not, there is one important point of commonality. Buddha, Freud, Erickson and Jung all used altered states of consciousness to heal the mind. What differed were primarily their specific methodologies. They all aimed at eradicating suffering.

The Buddha practiced and taught meditation to clear the mind of mental hindrances that caused negative repercussions in life.[45] His counterparts used hypnosis, psychoanalysis and other therapies, but they too sought to clear the mind of mental hindrances. They also used methods that caused a state of wonderment to occur, an altered state of consciousness.[46] This warrants classifying meditation,

hypnosis and psychotherapy as a trance-inducing mechanisms. A trance state is not mysticism but a natural psychological state of being.

The word "hypnosis" was first coined by a Scottish sur-
geon, James Braid, in 1841. He based his practices on those
developed by Franz Mesmer. The word is derived from the
Greek "hypnon," meaning the sleep of consciousness.[47] It is
after this time that scientists began to seriously study trance
states. As mentioned before, Freud, Milton Erickson[48] and
Jung all experimented with, borrowed from and developed
techniques of hypnosis.

For example, "[a]fter studying briefly with Bernheim,
Freud pioneered the use of hypnosis as a vehicle for regres-
sion and catharsis between about 1885 and 1905."[49] He then
developed psychoanalysis based on the knowledge he gained
from the study of hypnosis. In an article he published later,
Freud recounts the merging of hypnosis with psychoanalysis,

> *It might be necessary to somehow combine the findings
> of psychoanalysis with the methods of hypnotherapy in
> order to produce a briefer and more powerful form of
> treatment. This notion was subsequently developed by
> other psychotherapists and led to the school of hypnosis
> which we now call 'hypnoanalysis.'*[50]

Hypnosis is a way of accessing the unconscious mind,
a trance that alters our state of consciousness. Freud used
hypnosis because psychoanalysis is a hybrid form of hypnotherapy. Hypnosis, psychoanalysis, yoga and meditation
take different paths to the unconscious, but they all alter our
state of consciousness.

To make it easier to follow, from now on, when we say, "trance state," "mindfulness," "state of wonder," or "wonderment," we are referring to a state of mind that is different from our regular state of consciousness, one that is a bit more suggestible, a mental state in which intellectual activity takes a subordinate role to the unconscious, giving the conscious mind accesses to the unconscious.[31]

Spontaneous Trance States should be differentiated from Purposeful Trance States. Purposeful Trance States are induced for a purpose greater than achieving altered states of consciousness, usually to transform oneself.

Trance states may be as old as human consciousness. What is new is how we explain what states of wonder and mindfulness are. It is unlikely that all ancient people knew they were accessing an altered state of mind when they experienced a state of wonderment, entered trance states, or their mind wondered off somewhere else when they beheld the beauty of a sunset, or they looked too long into a camp fire. Some might have attributed such occurrences to magic or to supernatural beings.

> Over every culture and in every age, 'trance states' have been linked to healing....Although labeled differently and in different cultures and contexts, an altered state of awareness from our usual active and alert state of 'consciousness' is common to healing with peoples worldwide, and the similarities to what we are labeling 'hypnosis' are obvious.[51]

We know that yoga and meditation are millennia old. A steatite found at Mohenjo-Daro in the Indus Valley shows what archeologist and Director-General of the Archaeological Survey of India, Sir John Marshall, describes the "pose of a yogi … eyelids more than half closed … looking downward at the tip of the nose."[52] This is a typical meditation pose. Marshall dates this steatite to circa 3,250 BCE,[53] although some believe that the "Indus Valley (also known as the Harappan Civilization)" is much older and meditation was practiced even before such steatites were invented.

Whether or not one accepts that Harappan steatites are proof that meditation arose alongside civilization, many will agree that spiritual practices existed on every inhabited continent even before civilization and such practices induce trance state. It is easy to see that when ceremonies involving music, rhythmic dance and steady beats are performed, the audience and practitioners alike often enter a state of trance.

Perhaps what this means is that trance states are a natural human phenomena, practiced since the dawn of civilization, but have likely been misunderstood. Perhaps this shows that trance state is not a portal to gods and spirits but instead a doorway to the power of the unconscious mind. When used with purposeful intent to change our state of mind, an altered state of consciousness acts as a powerful *psychological* catalyst.

A Spiritual Monopoly

It is important to note that historically, techniques developed to induce trance states were hidden from or forbidden to the broader public. Trance states have historically been the domain of a limited group of "initiates," that is priests, monks, mystics, shamans and yogis. Sometimes exceptions occurred and sincere spiritual seekers were taught the mysteries, but this was not the norm. The everyday person was either too busy running the household or only allowed glimpses, mostly during public events and ceremonies and always under the guidance of an intermediary. Perhaps this is why, even today, meditation is a bit outside most cultural norms and has *not* been passed down from generation to generation among lay people.

This phenomenon did not just occur in the West. In the East, "In the distant past in order to have a 'true practice,' one was required to renounce the world and live one's life within the walls of a monastery or in the forest. To the lay person was left the observation of moral precepts, charity and devotion." Therefore, in ancient times, just as today, most ordinary people did not have the possibility of living a "committed spiritual life."[54]

Of course, things did not start out this way. It seems that time overturned our progress. According to my meditation teacher, the late S.N. Goenka, in his book *The Clock of Vipassana Has Struck*,

> As can be discerned from many of the Buddha's discourses, a great number of lay people who received the teaching of the practice in his time attained high levels of spiritual development ... From this, we can deduce that the Buddha himself did not intend to exclude lay people.[54]

In the West and the Middle East, Purposeful Trance state was usually practiced mostly at the church, the mosque or temple, and even then only for the purposes of worshipping God in an environment that was controlled by religious leaders. Most families have a tradition of ritualized prayer, a method of trying to communicate with their deity, but prayer does not usually produce the deep trance states characteristic of Eastern meditation. Prayers usually only last a few minutes and are not intended to make deep psychological changes, whereas meditation sessions often last an hour or more and are targeted to produce a deep effect.

Twenty-five hundred years after the Buddha, an interesting coincidence occurred. Buddhist monks such as Ledi Sayadaw (1846–1923) and Webu Sayadaw (1896–1977) started teaching mindfulness meditation, a secular, non-mystical form of meditation to lay people.[54] Some of the lay people they taught became respected meditation teachers in their own right, and then they too taught these techniques to others. During approximately the same time as the Sayadaws, Sigmund Freud and then later Carl Jung and Milton H. Erickson made accessing the unconscious mind available to the masses in the West, with the full blessings of science.

Why are these events important? The utmost goal of nineteenth century Western scientists and of ancient Buddhist masters was to help humanity actualize well-being, and both came to the same conclusion. The way to achieve inner peace is to access and change the processes of the mind. This was one of a few times in recorded history when humanity has set about accomplishing this task in a secular way, without turning to gods, supernatural forces or to magic. Now that the monopoly has been exposed, it is your turn to follow these first pioneers and to proceed on the path before you.

Pioneers of the Mind

The early pioneers of the mind left us a stunning challenge, the core of their message was, "Your life is pre-determined!"

Our lives *are* pre-determined, not by fate, nor by supernatural beings, but by the unconscious processes that reside within the empty self. *If* we do not learn to intercede into this shadowy world, we will continue to be driven by our instincts and emotions, until our fate is sealed.

Human beings have keen powers of observation and naturally develop an understanding of our world by observing the motion of life around us. We watch a warrior throw a spear and understand the power and motion of an arm muscle and the need for thrust and speed to overcome the pull of gravity on the spear in flight. But the anatomical structure of our brain sheds no obvious light on its function, and similarly, just thinking about thinking provides no obvious insights into the nature of thought.

Freud warned us of the unspeakable excesses of which humanity is capable, and spent a great deal of time showing us the influences that unconscious instincts have on us, if left unchecked. But even as soon as Freud started, others, including his former students, responded with their own warnings, developments and criticisms. These criticisms sounded as though they were conveying something different, but they all bore the same core message.

Jung strove to respect both the dark and the light facets of the human psyche; he saw an expansive vision where the human family moves forward in a continual cycle of evolution. His ultimate conclusion was,

Most people confuse 'self-knowledge' with knowledge of their conscious ego-personalities. Anyone
who has any ego-consciousness at all takes it for
granted that he knows himself. But the ego knows
only its own contents; not the unconscious."[5]

Jung further explained that many of our automatic
responses that lead to desperate lives are related to what he
called "unreflected beliefs," saying further, "belief is no ade-
quate substitute for inner experience."[56]

Erickson's view of the unconscious was utilitarian, and
through this he inspired other therapists who in turn helped
countless others. He mentored Margaret Meade, as well as
Richard Bandler and John Grinder, who were co-founders
of neuro-linguistic programming (NLP). He also collabo-
rated with Aldus Huxley on his research in altered states
of consciousness.[57] For his help and understanding of the
unconscious, Erickson received warm-hearted praise and
messages of sincere thanks from people all over the world.

According to his wife, the last letter he received before
he died was from Salvador Minuchin, the developer of
Structural Family Therapy. Starting off with pleasantries,
Minuchin says, "My meeting with you was one of those
memorable experiences. In my lifetime, I have met a hand-
ful of extraordinary people—you are one of them."

He then shares the gift Erickson gave him, "[I] was tre-
mendously impressed at your trust in the capacity of human
beings to harness a repertory of experiences they do not
know they have."[58]

We do have at our disposal a "repertory of experiences
that we do not know we have." Erickson saw the unconscious

as a positive transformative force that can overcome life's difficulties.[59] Even though he used methodologies different from those of Freud and Jung—going so far as to induce trance state during everyday situations and using metaphorical stories that acted as gentle nudges to the unconscious— his overall message was the same. Access the unconscious and transform your life.[57]

This is the same message delivered to us by one of the first pioneers of the mind. Siddhartha Gautama, too, saw the well-trained mind as an indispensable source of freeing oneself from suffering. He was convinced that *not meditating* and not fine-tuning the mind would leave it overburdened by the stresses of life, the vulnerabilities of being and attachments to illusory things that cause misery.[60]

He says, "[t]he wise person strengthens it [the mind] as a Fletcher straightens an arrow."[61] In the *Connected Discourses*, the Buddha poses a provocative question to us all. A modern rendering might sound like this:

Both a meditator and person who does not meditate feel pain, so why bother to meditate? How does training the mind through meditation help us?

An untrained mind *feels* pain but is unable to cope with it. Mental pain that we are unable to alleviate engenders suffering. This is like being shot twice with the same dart. Not knowing how to find peace within, the untrained mind delights in sensual diversions that cause attachment. Meanwhile, someone who meditates and trains the mind experiences pain abstractly and thus continues to dwell in inner peace.[62]

The Buddha, Freud, Jung, Erickson and many others, practiced different methodologies and disagreed with one another on many things, but their core point of agreement was their recognition of the power of the mind, both as a source of strength and suffering.

They recognized that, left alone, the unconscious sometimes makes us feel bad and makes us do things that we do not want to do and that there were often unconscious reasons for our behavior. Therefore, the most important lesson that we can learn from all their years of study is that it is essential to access the unconscious and untangle the negative patterns that reside within.

In order to preserve their collective experience, without being stuck with the baggage of any one school of thought, we will represent the essence of their work from an eclectic point of view, and we will use terminology that sounds somewhat similar to that used by Freud, Jung and others, but our terminology is simplified and divorced from any particular school of thought.

Because the following concepts describe the mind symbolically, they might seem unrelated to secular spirituality, secular meditation, or event to secularism. However, these concepts are fundamental to forming an outlook of life that is conducive to inner peace.

The human mind has a propensity towards superstition and tends to ascribe supernatural explanations to difficult or hard to understand experiences. Therefore, in the following chapters we will provide natural explanations for subjective phenomenon. But it is important to note that these descriptions are to be understood symbolically and that they do not endorse supernatural explanations.

Hypnosis A state of altered consciousness or trance.

Meditation Self-guided trance state; access to the unconscious mind for the purpose of changing or accessing unconscious mental processing.

Prayer A form of religious meditation, a trance state and form or self-hypnosis, externally or self-induced; the practice of communication with a perceived God, gods or other supernatural forces.

Chapter 7

The Unconscious Mind

*"People have a terrific loyalty to their brand of
cigarettes and yet in tests cannot tell it from other
brands. They are smoking an image, completely."*
—RESEARCH DIRECTOR, NEW YORK ADVERTISING
AGENCY, ON HOW UNCONSCIOUS IMPULSES
AFFECT OUR EVERYDAY LIVES

The mind allows us to understand, navigate through and
experience reality. It is composed of conscious and unconscious processes that facilitate all the functions of our lives.
Asked to describe it, we typically think of the unconscious as
a realm of instincts, like our instinct to move toward what
feels pleasant and away from what feels unpleasant. But our
unconscious mind is so much more than this. For most, it
is the seat of the conscience, of deep emotions, fantasies,
drives and automatic functions that cause events to occur
within our lives, underneath our awareness, like a subliminal robotic servant with sonar. The unconscious mind has

a much greater influence on our actions and thoughts than many people think.

Some might disagree and say they are fully in charge of their unconscious mind, their instincts and drives and that they don't need meditation. They know how to inspire themselves with common, everyday actions. Yet we have received plenty of examples to the contrary. People very rarely seem to understand their drives and motivations and what occurs within the mind.

Picture what might be the start of a typical day. You wake up in the morning feeling good, inspired by the faded memories of pleasant dreams, not exactly sure why you feel good. Then again, the opposite might be the case and you wake up feeling bad. You get out of bed, wash, get dressed and have breakfast, but this all happens automatically, in a daze, as a routine without much conscious effort, inspired by unconscious processes. Are you sure you are *fully* aware of what happens in your unconscious at all times?

If someone asks you to recall and describe your actions during each moment, you might find this difficult. Your conscious awareness has been drifting in and out throughout the morning. Or imagine the common aches and pains and disappointments you feel when things are not going according to your wishes. Who is it that sets your mood then? Do the aches and pains set the mood or the higher mind?

The Color Research Institute conducted an experiment, inviting a group of women to attend a lecture. They actually sought to observe their behavior while waiting. They gave them the option of using either of two waiting areas.

One was a functional modern chamber with gentle tones. It had been carefully designed for eye ease and to promote a relaxed feeling. The other room was a traditional room filled with period furniture, oriental rugs and expensive-looking wallpaper.

It was found that virtually all the women instinctively went into the Swedish modern room to do their waiting. Only when every chair was filled did the women start to overflow into the more ornate room.[64]

After the lecture, the ladies were asked, "'Which of those two rooms do you like better?' They looked thoughtfully [at pictures] of the two rooms, and then 84 percent said the period room was the nicer room."[64]

The fashion trends at that time dictated that the period room *was* nicer. And yet most chose to sit in the other room. Their conscious, intellectual mind was telling them that the expensive-looking period room *should* be the nicer room, but *unconsciously, they felt more comfortable in the functional modern chamber* (which, after all, the modern room was especially designed to promote a relaxed feeling). It turns out that until people learn how to be mindful of their internal world, they are generally unaware of what occurs in the preconscious and unconscious depths of their own minds.

American scientist, mathematician and philosopher Charles Sanders Peirce confirmed this in the nineteenth century, when he "discovered that the unconscious mind has knowledge unknown to the conscious."[63] In modern times, advertising executives, seeking to use the science

of motivational analysis and "to apply psychoanalytic techniques to market research," concluded that

> There are three main levels of interest to us. The
> conscious, rational level, where people know what
> is going on and are able to tell why.... The precon-
> scious and subconscious..., where a person may
> know in a vague way what is going on with his own
> feelings, sensations and attitudes but would not be
> willing to tell why. This is the level of prejudices,
> assumptions and fears, emotional promptings and
> so on. Finally, the third level is where we not only
> are unaware of our true attitudes and feelings but
> would not discuss them if we could.[64]

Our unconscious mind did not just start affecting us
when we were adults who were able to comprehend and give
consent to its workings. We are subject to the actions and
reactions of our inner depths even before we are born. In his
book, *Brandwashed*, Martin Lindstrom relates a Queens University study conducted in Belfast that,

> Newborn babies will actually show a preference for
> a TV theme...that was heard frequently by their
> mothers during pregnancy. [If a] mother heard
> a catchy jingle every day while pregnant and the
> mother had a pleasant or relaxing response to the
> jingle, the fetus, and then later the newborn, could
> have a conditioned response to the sound pattern
> and attend to it differently than other unfamiliar
> sounds. In other words, the minute we are born, we

may already be biologically programmed to like the sounds and music we are exposed to in utero.[65]

The effects of being unconscious to our environmental programming might bear sinister repercussions, even for the innocent. Based on the findings mentioned earlier, executives at a major chain of Asian shopping malls decided that they wanted to use such subliminal techniques to increase their sales. They played soothing music at their malls and used pleasant fragrances in stores frequented by unsuspecting pregnant mothers while they were shopping. According to later studies, not only did this boost sales, it yielded at least one unexpected result.

A year or so into the sensory experiment, the company began to be inundated by letters from mothers attesting to the spellbinding effect the shopping center had on their now newborns. Turns out the moment their babies entered the mall, they calmed down.... 60 percent of these women claimed they'd experienced this nowhere else, not even places where they were exposed to equally pleasant smells and sounds." Ominously, the unconscious minds of newborns had been conditioned by unscrupulous advertising techniques even before they were born! These babies, now children, were attached to the sounds and music played by stores when they were still in the womb![65]

Given cases like this, the basic precaution of meditation is more important than ever. It can help spur us to access

our unconscious reactions and predispositions daily, to
screen and monitor the social-cultural influences that the
environment imposes on us.

When I first started to study the unconscious mind in
the early 1990s, the "serious" scientific community seemed
to regard the subject as a taboo. Some people believed that
anything to do with the unconscious mind was pseudo-
scientific nonsense. "Odd as it might sound today, in the
first half of [the twentieth century], which was dominated
by those in the behaviorist movement, psychologists even
sought to do away with the concept of mind all together."[63]

Meanwhile, at the same time, advertisers paid no mind
and used these taboo techniques, making billions and changing the way masses of people thought and behaved. Hypno-
therapists experimented with these same taboo subjects and
yielded positive result for their clients. People who used
meditation also observed positive changes in their lives.
Since then, traditional conventions have caught up.

Unfortunately, in the past, these various disciplines
traditionally kept their findings to themselves. Each group
shunned the others, as if their practices were not related. Not
even Freud was immune to change. He seemed perplexed

> [t]hat his followers (Jung, Rank, Adler) had com-
> mitted the 'taboo' of differing with him, thereby
> challenging his (oedipal) authority. As a result, dur-
> ing the early decades of psychoanalysis, there was a
> lack of sanctioned opportunity to experiment, not
> only with changes in technique, but even with dif-
> ferent theoretical formulations.[66]

Perhaps this initial approach explains some of

the resistance we have seen in the scientific community in the early years.

Fortunately, it now looks like various taboos are being lifted. "Today, it is much more permissible for analysts to expand, extend, alter, or replace aspects of psychoanalytic theories, but changes in technique are [still] frowned upon."[66]

Scientists can now seriously study the unconscious mind without being accused of practicing pop psychology and are even performing studies and experiments to test the benefits of the other disciplines. For example, respected universities such as UCLA are sponsoring conferences such as "Buddhism and Psychotherapy"[66] to study the benefits of meditation.

Let us hope this trend continues, with the exception that media and advertising organizations seem already to have enough "unconscious mind technology," and so should curtail using their high-tech hypnotic powers on the unsuspecting public.

Therefore, in the spirit of understanding the nuances of the unconscious in order to benefit from the knowledge and experience gained over the centuries, we will view the mind from an eclectic perspective; we will use the terms unconscious and subconscious interchangeably and in a non-Freudian sense, and not associate these terms with any particular school of psychology. Consider the following descriptions of the unconscious in order to get a better understanding of the inner depths and functions of the mind.

Functions of the Unconscious Mind

The unconscious mind is both dumb and wise. Dumb because some functions of the mind are machine-like. Wise because it is responsible for our ingenious creativity and inspiration. It feeds information to the conscious mind, it inspires us, and it serves as the means to attain inner peace. We can grasp these different functions more easily if we think in terms of Higher and Lower Unconscious.

The Higher Unconscious is responsible for emotions, inspiration, subconscious will and subconscious modes of communication. It is generally accessed by consciousness quite easily, and so Freud calls this the preconscious,[67] but we do not use this term because it is too rigid and does not take into account some of the findings we discuss herein.

Meanwhile, the Lower Unconscious is the automatic, reactionary part of the mind that is responsible for unconscious urges and desires, instincts and passions. The Lower Unconscious serves a purely reactionary purpose, including, among others, biological functions such as breathing and swallowing.

Even though the Lower Unconscious is integrated with every part of the body, keeping us alive and well, its mechanisms are nonetheless automatic and reactionary. In this most basic capacity, the Lower Unconscious serves as an autopilot for the body and a control mechanism for all our important biological processes. It works behind the scenes and leaves the consciousness mind free to do its job. Freud called this part of the mind the id,[68] but again, our use of this concept is much more varied and so we do not use Freud's term.

Does the mind make mistakes, or do mistakes happen

for our own unconscious reasons? This is a great question, one that will probably be debated for ages to come. Either there are random occurrences, some good and some bad, or the mind has an unseen, unconscious plan and so "mistakes" are simply parts of the plan unknown to the intellect.

Chapter 8

The Conscious Mind

If, as many psychologists and philosophers believe, we establish the importance of the human psyche by stating with Jung that, "Man's capacity for consciousness alone makes him man,"[148] then we should come to terms with how consciousness affects our view of reality and how this affects the totality of the mind.

By "mind" I mean the totality of our conscious and unconscious mental processes,[69] meaning that the two are what make up *how we see reality.*

Perhaps this is why Dr. Wayne Dyer says, "The state of your life is nothing more than a reflection of your state of mind."[146] As you use the tools suggested in this book, rather than being driven by culture, environment and automatic reactions, you will learn to comprehend your perceptions and unconscious drives in new ways and be empowered to re-program the conditioning that limits you. This is the essence of being spiritually secular.

It is important to understand that anything we are conscious of *is* the function of the conscious mind. The conscious mind thinks and reasons, analyzes and forms concepts, solves problems, gathers information, and further interprets the data, making judgments.[71] In this way, it is a gatekeeper of reality, our final version of perception. It manages our lives and maps our progress in relation to our known goals, dreams, desires and views of the world, keeping a pulse on progress or lack thereof. But it is also limited and sometimes forced to cater to unconscious reactions.

The conscious mind is most often perceived as being identical to the intellect, and the unconscious as merely its shadow, some sort of separate, mystical offshoot of consciousness.[55] But in reality, we would still be able to exist without our type of conscious mind; many animals do. The human intellect is, relatively speaking, a recent evolutionary upgrade. When we consider our conscious mind as a biological adaptation, it is easy to see its advantages. It increases our functionality, in large part by improving our capacity to manipulate our environment.[63] It gives us self-knowing, the ability to see ourselves as others might see us, the ability to plan, to imagine the future and invent fantasy scenarios, as well as to revisit the past.

Think of conscious as being a sort of director and journalist that, at the same time, gets its information from a vast resource, the unconscious. The unconscious is connected to all our happenings, internal and external. We do not actually see the world directly. The brain receives electro-chemical impulses and unconsciously translates this "data" into useful and meaningful information (usually).

In effect, this journalist and director, the unconscious mind, is making sense out of the data for us without our conscious awareness, and thus the mind is forming a particular view of reality for us. This view becomes *our* view of existence, whether it is correct or not. The conscious mind then produces further meaning from the data we receive.[63]

Without the intellect, we would respond to stimuli mostly through instinct quickly, automatically and efficiently enough for survival, but we would not be able to ponder those deeper questions, make rational and analytic choices, or build complex tools, social structures, or civilizations.

Thinking about rational choices and instinct reminds me of Las Vegas—but not for the reasons you might imagine. We once lived close enough to Vegas to be able to visit whenever we wanted. Besides the hotels, the lights and the sparkle of the strip, what also stood out for me were the large colorful billboards and marquees. I remember in particular one of Siegfried & Roy's billboards. It featured the two "master illusionists" dressed in glitz-sparkled white jumpsuits and standing alongside white tigers with deadly, piercing eyes. It was the most popular show in the history of the city, and it symbolized the thrill and glam of Vegas.[72]

According to Alan Nash's *Reader's Digest* article,

> Roy didn't so much train the animals as bond with them through a technique he called 'affection conditioning,' raising tiger cubs from birth and sleeping with them until they were a year old … Siegfried and Roy lived with them … Roy meditated with at least one tiger every day. 'When an animal gives you

its trust,' Roy had said, 'you feel like you have been given the most beautiful gift in the world.'[73]

But somehow, I never got to see the show. Years later, while flipping channels, I heard the shocking news. Roy lay near death. During a show, Montecore, a seven-year-old, 380-pound white Bengal tiger had become distracted and started to walk menacingly toward the audience. Roy stopped him, but in the process dropped the tiger's chain. Trying to free the chain, Roy commanded, "Release! Release!"[73]

After a bit of a struggle,

Montecore relaxed his grip, but Roy had been straining to pull away, and fell backward over the tiger's leg. In an instant, Montecore was on top of him, clamping his powerful jaws around Roy's neck…crushing his windpipe…The tiger was resolute, and dragged him 30 feet offstage 'literally like a rag doll,' as another witness recalls…The tiger had torn Roy's jugular vein, barely missing the carotid artery…Animal behaviorists say it's likely that Montecore was on his way to delivering a killing bite, much as a tiger in the wild would, to bring down an antelope."[73] Kay Rosaire, who runs the Big Cat Encounter, a show near Sarasota, Florida, said, "Even though they're raised in captivity and they love us, sometimes their natural instincts just take over.[73]

Siegfried and Roy insist that the tiger realized something

was wrong and was trying to protect Roy by dragging him off stage, just as a momma does to a cub when it is in trouble. He only accidently severed Roy's vein, not realizing that carrying Roy would injure him. Either way, rather than reasoning and considering all the dangers and implications, a tiger reacts instinctively, either to kill its prey or to save its loved ones.

What makes humans different is our conscious mind. We have the ability to think and reason before we act (even though we sometimes fail to do so), and we have the ability to override our natural instincts and re-wire our (otherwise) unconscious reactions. Big cats and other animals do not have these same abilities. They react more instinctually.

Limitations of the Conscious Mind

> "The subliminal aspects of everything that happens to us may seem to play very little part in our everyday lives. But they are the almost invisible roots of our conscious thoughts."
> —SIGMUND FREUD.

Ironically, the conscious mind's greatest ability is also perhaps its greatest limitation. The intellect too often mistakes its own perceptions for facts, as if its perceptions were unlimited and all-knowing. And yet its perceptions and memory are *extremely limited*. What we see, hear and remember is *not complete,* and yet we usually believe our perceptions. Does this mean belief is overrated? In his book *How Your Unconscious Mind Rules Behavior*, Leonard Mlodinow demonstrates this and reminds us that "[t]he human sensory system sends the brain about eleven million bits of information each second... The conscious mind cannot process near that amount. The actual amount of information we can handle has been estimated to be somewhere between sixteen and fifty bits per second."[63]

This low processing rate saves the intellect from being overwhelmed with too much information, but as a result, consciousness perceives an incomplete picture of reality. To make up for incomplete data, the mind unconsciously fills in the gaps with imagination. This is such an important point that I am going to repeat it: the mind imagines reality to make up for gaps in its awareness! Therefore, in our perception of every moment, there are blocks of data that are missing and other pieces of data that are made up.[63]

There are at least two dangers when we rely only on our conscious mind awareness. One is that we might misperceive our current reality due to an inability to connect with a deeper understanding of what exists at any given point in time. The other danger is one of omission: we become so focused on surface changes that we fail to perceive ongoing but important truths about the world around us. As Alan Watts explains:

It is characteristic of consciousness that it ignores stimuli that are constant. When anything is constant, consciousness says 'Okay, that's safe. I needn't pay attention to that anymore.' And therefore, we systematically eliminate from our awareness all the gorgeous things that are going on all the time, and instead, we focus only on the troublesome things that might upset us.[74]

This is a danger because the more we do this, the more we identify with what is near that may be problematic and the less we have time to think about existing conditions that nurture us.

Naturally, the omissions and distortions of each individual consciousness are often sources of apparently conflicting views among different people. How we view reality is also affected by the capabilities and limits of our senses, our state of health (both psychological and physical), our past experience and beliefs and our mood and level of education.

Without the unconscious, we would just be processing uninspired information. Without consciousness, we would be feeling and reacting without fully understanding our reactions or being able to do anything about them. We create our greatest works when inspiration coming from the unconscious mind is coupled with our conscious-mind abilities. One can perhaps say that the unconscious mind originates humanity's genius, our invention, art and the amazing things we create, and consciousness materializes them. Even so, the mind is often pulled in different directions by unconscious needs and drives and by the ego. Freud likened this to "[a] man on horseback, who has to hold in check the superior strength of the horse."[67] This is why it is so important to understand our programming and to know how to counteract its effects.

Chapter 9

Accessing the Unconscious

"What lies behind us and what lies before us are tiny matters compared to what lies within us."
—RALPH WALDO EMERSON

How does it feel to make a voyage into the unconscious? The beginning of the 1990s marked a new beginning in my life. Standing on a Corpus Christi beach in Texas on the morning after an all-night party, I stared at the rolling waves. They seemed like different states of mind, cascading possibilities. A waterfall of questions churned my mind. I wondered if it was possible for *me* to learn to be free, without all that outward struggle that sweeps away so many lives. Could *I* access the unconscious and become independent of external things? I wondered at the purpose of my life, of what would happen to me after death and if meditation could free me from suffering.

I contemplated the words I had just recently read in a tattered book I'd found somewhere. The book had seen better days and would soon be discarded, but the words were true, spoken by the Buddha almost three thousand years ago, "We are what we think. All that we are arises with our thoughts. With our thoughts, we make our world."[112] Would I be able to change the reactions of the mind and change my fate? What we think does create our behavior and habits, character and current state of being. But do our thoughts truly change our lives?

I resolved to visit several Buddhist temples to find out, to learn meditation. But what I found disappointed me. The temples I visited were dedicated to religion, ceremony and tradition. Perhaps the techniques were there in the scriptures and maybe even in the hearts and minds of people who practiced the essence of the *dhamma*. Unfortunately, what I found was that the lay people I met were more into venerating the monks and religious leaders, following temple regulations and ceremonies than seeking enlightenment. Meanwhile, they preferred to leave meditation, the key component to enlightenment, to the professionals and practiced it sparingly. In this way, even nontheistic religions that are based on Internal Sources of happiness are sometimes too concentrated on Externals! Not being a Buddhist monk, I was not allowed into the inner sanctum of the deeper knowledge. So for me, traditional Buddhism was steeped with too many cultural associations, rites, rituals and even supernatural beliefs. I did not yet know about Secular Buddhism.

Perhaps this is the problem that sometimes occurs. Followers stop emulating the thoughts and actions of the founder and begin to worship the figurehead, building institutions that keep the organization alive but kill its spirit. It is then that worship and creed become more important than practice.

Within a year of standing on that beach, I came across a means to learn more. I saw an advertisement for a year-long program leading to certification in the field of Clinical Hypnotherapy. At first, I nearly brushed it off, quick to equate hypnosis with stage magic. I was not interested in magic or parlor tricks. But something deeper motivated me to research further.

I do not now see hypnotherapy as the best solution to enact Inner-Actualization, because it requires external help. For this reason, I prefer the grounding that an inner source-oriented meditation technique provides. However, learning hypnotherapy helped me to better understand how the mind functions, and I recognized that it can serve as an aid or motivator.

Hypnotherapy uses hypnosis which can be used for entertainment, to help people, or even to take advantage of people. Of course, this made me a bit leery of hypnosis, but I will tell you later how to best protect yourself against such things. Hypnotherapy is different; it specifically aims to help people change their limiting behavior and overcome fears, to achieve desired goals—usually external goals.[58] It is administered with the expressed permission of the participant and is a scientific discipline. In the United States, the field of hypnotherapy is overseen by national organizations that certify their members, requiring adherence to strict ethical codes of conduct, continued proficiency and education.

Trance States

Hypnotherapy taught me about trance states, which can be helpful to anyone, so I will share this information with you.

Altered states of consciousness are so common that we often fail to notice them. For instance, anytime intellectual activity is diminished and takes a subordinate role to the unconscious—when we space out, daydream, become inspired or experience a state of wonder—we are in an altered state of consciousness. "Altered state of consciousness," "a state of wonderment," "trance state" and "hypnosis"[114] all mean roughly the same thing.[46] Therefore, every healthy individual accesses the unconscious mind daily.[113]

How do we know altered states of consciousness occur? An exchange of chemicals in the neural pathways generates electrical activity in the brain. This can be measured in several different ways.

Consciousness, the Beta state, shows an EEG reading frequency of 14–35 Hz cycles per second.[93] When in this state, the mind serves us as a gatekeeper, screening and filtering the information we receive, fact-checking against our database of stored knowledge, experiencing perceived reality. Below this, we enter trance state.

During trance or Alpha state, the mind slows to 8–13 Hz and drifts into an in-between state, interfacing with the deeper levels of the mind, able to affect our programming.[93] Even though our character and moral principles continue to be active and we are still conscious, we are tuned out, no longer screening every bit of information. The gatekeeper of consciousness rests, stepping aside to a certain extent, no longer choosing between fact or fiction. It is not thinking critically now, and thus we are more suggestible because the information we now receive is believable, whether it is true or not.

We enter this hypnotic state quite often, even during everyday activities, while listening to music, watching TV, exercising and even while at church or temple or when doing activities that require our attention. Think about the last time you drove a car or motorcycle. Do you remember every second of your journey? There were times when the mind drifted off, the unconscious took over and drove the car for you. Maybe you caught yourself, realizing you had drifted off somewhere. You were conscious, yet within the unconscious.[115] Drugs and alcohol are other instances when we experience trance state, even though chemically induced trance state debilitates, rather than pacifies the intellect.[116]

Most people love being in a state of wonderment, a trance state. Call to mind the best movies, music, art, sermons, lectures, drugs and alcohol: *they make you forget the moment*. You become lost in what you are experiencing and forget about everyday reality. The conscious mind slips away. You become transformed into what you are watching or listening. You lose track of time and self. We cannot live without altered states. The conscious mind needs to withdraw and rest, recharge and reflect. Just like with an overheated computer processor, sometimes we need to *power down* the mind.

Theta range, at a frequency of 4–7 Hz., straddles trance state and light sleep. If you go deep enough, past trance state, your brain waves slow down, and you enter the dream state. Consciousness withdraws and the gatekeeper dozes off and fights imaginary battles. The consciousness that remains helps us to remember our dreams. If we go deeper than dream state, Delta range, .5–4 Hz., control is gone.[93]

How does this relate to meditation? fMRI neuroimaging studies confirm that "meditation produces activity in the prefrontal cortex, the right anterior insula, and right hippocampus."[117] Meditation calms the mind to 4–13 Hz per second. This shows that meditation is/induces a purposeful state of trance. If used correctly, it reduces suffering and produces well-being. To maximize its benefits it is important to know the difference between Spontaneous and Purposeful Trance states.

Spontaneous and Purposeful Trance

I was astounded when I learned about trance states. I am a dreamer. I go into that "space" all the time. People who have observed this about me sometimes ask, "You just got lost in thought. Where did you go?"

Before I formally studied the mind, I did not know how to answer these questions. I did not realize that I was entering an altered state of consciousness and did not know what trance was. I did not even realize that there were benefits to entering a different state of mind. Later, I learned that when we access trance states, we access the unconscious mind, experiencing inner peace and often becoming inspired, insightful and motivated to enact personal change. When I thought about it, excepting supernatural experiences, this is what people claim occurs when they are being "spiritual."

What if trance state is spirituality? What if spirituality is a psychological state of being, the innate awareness that occurs when the conscious mind accesses the unconscious mind? What if the mind gives us access to our greatest potential, and spirituality means being in touch with that potential?

There are two major ways to enter trance state: purposefully or spontaneously. Spontaneous Trance State or spontaneous mindfulness is a trance state that is undirected or uncontrolled. Purposeful Trance State or purposeful mindfulness is a trance state that is achieved intentionally and it is self-controlled. It uses a mechanism such as meditation to allow access to unconscious mind.

When we enter Spontaneous Trance States we receive insights, but these insights are random, uncontrolled and usually in the form of incomplete symbols, emotions, or visual cues. Thus, the inspiration and cues produced by a Spontaneous Trance State do not yield as beneficial an insight as do purposeful states, since they are not as easy to interpret correctly. The information that we get from them is often vague, unrecognizable and easy to misunderstand. Spontaneous Trace State is not to be confused with meditation on "nothingness," as the latter is still a purposeful form of meditation.

We frequently think our beliefs are self-created and our taste is individually conceived and unique. This is true to some extent; however, much of what we believe and do comes from environmental conditioning. There is a reason why people from the same environment generally like similar foods, types of music, and styles of clothing and have similar religious beliefs. This is the most shocking aspect of how unconscious conditioning works. To lesser or greater extents, our beliefs are ingrained in us by our cultural setting. Even when we leave our culture, move to another country, or change our environment and have new choices, the old conditioning can battle the new, and in the end, the old programming often proves impervious to the new—unless we re-evaluate our programming and change it from within.

Therefore, no matter how pleasant, relaxing or insightful it can be, a Spontaneous Trance State is not the best way to access the unconscious. It is not enough.

A Purposeful Trance State allows us to observe unconscious processes in a rational way, to re-wire the brain and overcome our limitations. The science of neuroplasticity shows that when we are in trance state, the physical structures of the brain actually change to accommodate our intended purpose.[1] By overwriting the tendency towards pessimism, the act of using neural techniques that encourage optimistic thinking can defeat the brain's bias towards pessimism, resulting in better overall well-being.

Being able to intentionally access the unconscious is one of our greatest assets and one the best advantages of being human because it puts this power in our hands. This type of spirituality is free of beliefs and gives us access to inner peace, allowing us to re-program our limitations. It gives us the ability to evaluate the ways in which we are affected by everyday happenings, culture and society, and to point our mind toward the ultimate goal.

What is the best way to purposefully enter trance state, and what do we do once we are in trance state? I have found that the most powerful mechanism for this purpose is some type of secular meditation that concentrates on Internal Sources, but it was with great difficulty that I found this answer. This is how that journey unfolded.

Chapter 10

Voyage Beyond the Self

*"I went to the woods because I wished to live
deliberately, to front only the essential facts of life, and
see if I could not learn what it had to teach, and not,
when I came to die, discover that I had not lived."*
—HENRY DAVID THOREAU

After a year of non-stop learning about the unconscious mind, I graduated, earning certification in clinical hypnotherapy. I was elated, ready to help people to achieve their goals. But as I began working with clients, I soon realized that people were not aware that behind their goals of losing weight, quitting smoking, improving self-esteem, enhancing success and overcoming phobias, there lurked deeper issues, masked by symptoms and smoke screens. Worse still, hypnotherapy must stay on good terms with the ego personality, the very mechanism that causes much of the trouble. Often, it is the ego that sets goals, pretends to want a cure and brings the individual to therapy.

A man harbors deep-seated feelings of worthlessness.

He comes to see me. His ego tells him that he would feel better if he bought himself a shiny new boat. He buys the boat to feel more successful, cannot afford the payments, and can hardly afford his bills. He wants me to help him, but he is not ready to confront his deep-seated issues. Hypnotherapy gives him a mirror into which he is not prepared to gaze.

Hypnotherapy is amazingly effective in achieving Self-Actualization. It re-programs the mind according to the wants of the intellect. A good hypnotherapist will work to expose hidden motivations and heal the unhealthy ego, dancing with it but not quite catering to its desires, and will sometimes give the client his own tools to use. But as the Buddha said, so often and in so many ways, goals that involve Externals strengthen the ego, causing attachment and compounding our suffering.

The disadvantage of hypnotherapy is that the ego personality can hijack, delay or stop the work. Meditation does not have this disadvantage because when done properly, it shunts the ego personality aside, pacifying it to sleep. These realizations led me to formulate the basic theoretical concepts that I would later call Inner-Actualization, but I needed to do more research. When I first set out to learn hypnotherapy, one of my goals was to work on my own issues, but as a hypnotherapist, I found little time. I soon felt the need to start again. After a while, it became apparent that my favorite method of working on myself was meditation, not hypnotherapy, and this is also what I recommended to others. This was the beginning of the end of my hypnotherapy career.

Until then, my life had been concentrated outward, trying to gain satisfaction by external means. But this did not work and wrapped me tighter in life's golden chains. I wanted to learn a technique that was effective in helping me to re-program the mind, bypassing the ego and achieving inner satisfaction. Having thought about spirituality, I also needed to determine for myself what religion meant to me. What was my hypothesis regarding what occurred after death?

Regarding religion, is it more probable that we wind up in Heaven or Hell, under the tutelage of God or the devil (Abrahamic Theism)? Or, are there multiple sets of heavens and hells, staffed by many gods, where reincarnation prevails (Hindu Theism)? Or, maybe traditional Buddhism is correct? I am referring to the type of Buddhism that is Spiritual Nontheism, which is not infiltrated by theism. It believes in rebirth: we just *are*—a continuous changing wave of cause and effect. We generate our own peace or suffering, based on our own actions. There is no God to save us because He does not exist. Or maybe Materialism is true, and we simply cease to exist after death? We are the body, star stuff, and there is nothing more to it than that.

I resolved to search for answers, to learn to meditate and find out for myself and to travel around the world, visiting those places that birthed the different paths, religions and secular ideas.

At the time, I did not know that no one really *knew* what occurred after death and that we were all just guessing. The reason this was so difficult to figure out was because people spoke with such conviction—little did I know that their convictions were driven by faith, not by incontrovertible evidence, and that they equated faith with fact.

To make the journey possible, for the sake of economy and of not having to worry about anything back home, I sold or gave away everything that I owned. At first, my only travel companion was a backpack stuffed with a few belongings. Originally, I intended to sail around the world with my girlfriend and best friend. However, my friends chose to pursue different paths. I regret not travelling with them, but in looking back, I realize that we make important choices on an unconscious level and that there are deeper reasons for our actions.

My journey began, and I literally headed to the farthest reaches of the earth. I lived without permanent shelter, safety net or conveniences, for nearly three years. The road was often my only companion. Too many times, when things seemed alarming, everything fell into place, the way it did one night on a back road to a nameless city in Turkey. The night was cold and damp. Shadows made me think of hooded beings lying in wait. I had the feeling that if I disappeared, walking down that dirt road, my family and friends would likely never find out what had happened to me. But soon, experiences like this made me smile, as there was a certain edge to them. For some reason, I knew everything would be okay.

I had no encumbrances or allegiances to any particular path, religion or philosophy. I tried what came my way. I wanted to know the truth, so I followed wherever the Universe took me. I often asked fellow travelers "Have you come across anything here that affected you deeply? Have you met any particular teacher that I should meet or learn from?" I sought out every philosopher, deep person and spiritual soul I could find. Often my travels took me to the very places where the religions and spiritual paths originated.

Sometimes I felt like one of the characters in Jack

Kerouac's novel *The Dharma Bums*. Other books of this type that inspired me and put me in the right frame of mind were *Siddhartha,* by Herman Hesse; *Walden*, by Henry David Thoreau; books by Mahatma Gandhi; some of Leo Tolstoy's philosophical books like *A Confession and other Religious Writings*; and the nineteenth-century book written by an anonymous Russian author, *The Way of a Pilgrim.*

Traveling this way was a great exercise in simple living. All I owned were the clothes on my back and some necessities. My money was a limited resource and could run out at any time. I sustained myself on the most basic of food, shelter and clothing. I ate mostly vegan meals. I did my best not to be attached to material things, to see what life was like raw and fresh, and I tried to *just be*. It is at this time that I met my wife and soul mate, who joined me on this journey.

I noted my experiences in twenty one-inch thick journals. I plan on reliving the adventures of the trip around the world with you one day. For now, it is important to share the results of my research into and experimentation with the practice of Inner-Actualization.

A Place to Learn

History is full of examples of people who learned to "go within," to access the power of the unconscious mind and to achieve great results. There is no reason to re-invent the wheel for this. There are methodologies that have been used successfully for thousands of years. My goal at that time was to find the most effective methods.

Because I was a certified hypnotherapist, I already knew how to access the unconscious mind, but unfortunately,

methods used by hypnotherapy relied on the hypnotherapist and were therefore External Sources. I needed to
find an internal method, one that did not rely on others. I
knew I could not learn this from most religions, as religions
also used External Sources. They relied on intermediaries,
priests, pastors, holy books and supernatural entities.

I was looking for a universal path that could be practiced by religious and non-religious people alike, so once I
helped myself I could help others. I could not use the tools
that were used by the self-help and positive-thinking movements either, because in practice, these movements were
focused on helping people achieve a type of Self-Actualization and usually did not understand the difference between
relying on External and Internal Sources.

Eventually, I found myself in India, with its long history of teaching the "inner arts." There are even some who
speculate that Jesus Christ spent his "lost years" in India and
developed his special powers there.[118] I decided to look for a
proper meditation center to learn a technique. I had specific
criteria for what I expected from a genuine technique and
from a meditation center that would facilitate Inner-Actualization. These requirements were non-negotiable.

First, the meditation center had to teach a viable and
proven technique that accessed the unconscious mind and
achieved inner peace. Second, the technique itself could
not rely on External Sources such as audio tapes, machines,
other people, things or beings. Third, the technique had to
make sense scientifically and not be based on the mystical
or supernatural. Fourth, the meditation center was not to
be religious, or tied to some sect or religious organization.
I was not there to learn religion, or to join an organization

for the sake of furthering their aims. My aim was to learn a technique that would help me and others find inner peace. Fifth, I did not want to join some cult or money-grubbing racket.

I tested several meditation centers and techniques to evaluate whether or not they met my criteria. One of my tests was to determine whether an organization was more interested in me or my money. I walked away from organizations and gurus that did not meet these criteria. Many did not seem right. I knew that my requirements were stringent. I was not even sure if what I was looking for existed, but I did my best to find out. In the end, one center met all my criteria, and since then I've heard of others.

One day a traveler told me about a likely place. To paraphrase him, "This place is for real. They are not interested in money. They don't force you to convert to some religion. What they teach is scientific and it works. Go meet with S.N. Goenka. He is at his meditation center right now, and he teaches *vipassana*, a technique that has been practiced successfully for more than 2,500 years. Even though it was developed by the Buddha, it is not textbook Buddhism like the religion. Check it out!"

Well, I did. I looked at a pamphlet produced by the center and laughed. Remember how in the beginning of the book I told you that I agreed with what the Buddha taught, but that some Buddhist temples taught a religion instead of his methods? Well, here was a place that taught mindfulness, a secular meditation technique that could achieve the same level of inner peace as Inner-Actualization. It taught a simple process that used the natural reactions of the body and the unconscious mind, and it did not rely on religion.

Looking into it further, this was a place where I could experiment with Inner-Actualization, in the field. The centers were not perfect—most institutions are not—but they met my criteria, and the techniques they taught did work. I find this to be the case even after nearly two decades of personal experience with this organization and from the experiences of others who have tried the technique.

The Methodology

Now that we understand the theoretical advantages of Inner-Actualization, the reasons for moving beyond the empty self and breaking our golden chains, it makes sense to try the antidote in real life. Otherwise, it is just a theoretical ideal, a pipedream. What we need to keep working on is shattering our illusions, those often managed by the ego. More specifically, we can learn to re-program the negativities of mind that keep us stressing and suffering.

There are some misconceptions about meditation. Some think that meditation is a means to gain magical powers or to access supernatural happiness or that it is some sort of mystical entertainment. Others think of meditation as some sort of supernatural telephone that gives us access to external beings that magically rescue us from our cares. Still others see meditation as an end in and of itself, a magic pill, to get "in the zone." They think that meditation *is* instantaneously inner peace; that we sit down, meditate and get bliss. None of these misconceptions are true.

I had no illusions about quick fixes. Inner-Actualization is a serious process that takes time to implement. Our current psychological state of being results in thinking that causes us to suffer. Proper meditation unravels the thinking that causes suffering. It takes time to un-program the negative patterns that have built up in the mind. The idea is not to sit down and purify the mind in one swoop. One works to eliminate the mental patterns that cause unnecessary stress, slowly, one by one. Some believe that this takes lifetimes or that there really is no possibility other than to keep doing what you are doing and to keep suffering.

A proper meditation technique helps us achieve Inner-Actualization. It is not itself Inner-Actualization. Peering into the unconscious is not usually a pleasant experience, especially at first. It forces us to confront the negativities that people ordinarily divert their attention from. This is why, for so many, meditation is the most difficult thing they will ever do in their lives. However, until we confront and purify our negative habit patterns, we will continue to suffer. Proper meditation calms the conscious mind, gives us access to the unconscious and then allows us to work on those psychological patterns that lead to misery.

Chapter 11

Free Will and Suffering

"We have not to risk the adventure alone, for the heroes of all time have gone before us. The labyrinth is thoroughly known. We have only to follow the thread of the hero path."
—JOSEPH CAMPBELL

What is missing from your life? Are you in charge of your body and mind, the hero of your life story? Or are you pushed and pulled by external forces, like a puppet, resigned to your fate? Where is your free will?

Harnessing free will to break the chains of human suffering is one of the most pervasive and enduring challenges in human history. In most depictions, a cultural hero figure is called to action by some unbearable condition—often represented by a monster, beast, dragon or demon. This hero figure is what Jung calls an "archetype,"[111] and it represents the very challenge that we face. Appearing multiple times across many cultures, these ancient images have resided in our unconscious minds for eons, often appearing in our dreams, witch doctors or described in war stories told by chieftains around blazing campfires.

We could choose just about any hero from classical literature and then reference similar tales of gallantry and gumption at other points in time. Let's consider the medieval folktale of St. George and the dragon. In a small village by a lake, farmers had to surrender their sheep to feed a dragon that lived in the lake. When they ran out of sheep, in desperation, they offered up their children by lottery, until one day the lot fell upon the daughter of a nearby king. Just as she was to be offered to the monster, St. George charged the dragon with his lance and trampled the fallen serpent with his white horse.

But the tale of the dragon slayer goes back to the founding origins of Delphi, where Apollo slew the drakon, Pythos; to Norse myths, where Thor defeats a snake-like beast, and the Book of Revelation, where an evil dragon holds forth, chapter after chapter. We can see the figure of the dragon as representing a problematic aspect of our unconscious and the warrior is the element of our psyche that rescue us from suffering.

A hero is "someone who has given his or her life to something bigger than oneself," according to Joseph Campbell. "Whether his heroic deed is physical or psychic, great courage is required to meet the challenge."[2]

Jung believed the idea of Christ the Redeemer has parallels with other pre-Christian lore, where a hero rescuer is devoured by a monster but then appears again in a miraculous way. Then the hero defeats the whale/dragon. With so many generations of retelling, Jung said, "We can safely assume that the motif originated at a time when man did not yet know that he possessed a hero myth."[55] The hero figure is a typical image, an archetype that has existed since time immemorial.

There is great staying power in the core mythologies of the hero. George Lucas consulted with Joseph Campbell as he was writing the *Star Wars* trilogy. Campbell helped inspire some of the film's messages. In an interview with Bill Moyers, Campbell pointed out how Luke Skywalker served as an agent of our intuition rather than a promoter of galactic technology:

> It's what Goethe said in *Faust* but which Lucas has dressed in modern idiom—the message that technology is not going to save us. Our computers, our tools, our machines are not enough. We have to rely on our own intuition, on our true being.[2]

And when Luke must face the high-tech brutality of his Darth Vader nemesis, Campbell noted that "[b]y overcoming the dark passions, the hero symbolizes our ability to control the irrational savage within us."[2]

We are born to be the heroes of our lives, but because of the unconscious nature of the subconscious mind, sometimes the body does not comply with our wishes. We determine that certain behavior is good yet fail to do it. We decide that other behavior is bad, but we do it anyway. Think of how many tries it takes to achieve the simplest of goals. We make up New Year's resolutions and then do not live by them. We promise often things to our spouses, friends, children and even to ourselves and fail to do them. We fall into addictions ranging from drugs, to alcohol, to food, to sex and so many other things. This is the case for most of humanity. How many thousands of laws, commandments, ethical rules and personally created goals has humanity broken, accidentally or deliberately?

We are continually receiving a vast quantity of information from every direction, including TV, radio, the Internet, books, religion, society, political sources, friends and family. Amid this information assault, a certain percent of the messages that we are exposed to make it past our conscious filters and become seated in our unconscious minds. These messages can become our beliefs, whether true or not and whether we would consciously choose to believe them or not.

Our unfamiliarity with the subliminal explains why advertising is a multi-billion dollar industry: it works. We "buy" some of the information we receive—and not always while using our higher mind. It seems advertisers are well aware of the power they have over us and of their ability to influence our hearts, sometimes with messages they know to be at most half-truths.

It is important to be aware that our unconscious mind performs actions on our behalf—it makes choices automatically, and our bodies act. After the fact, our conscious mind winds up wondering what happened. Our actions and thoughts are subject to the power of our emotions, impulses, dreams and beliefs. Our environment influences us through the unconscious mind, and these influences can bypass our intellect's ability to judge fact from fiction.

The interesting question is whether cultural and political conditioning occurs in our acquisition of religious beliefs. Is this why most people in the Middle East are Muslim, in the West either Christian or Atheist, and in India Hindu? Is this why in Russia, before communism, most people were Orthodox Christian. After communism fell, people once again turned to religion.[119]

In the great scheme of things, cultural programming is an important concept to understand. Learning how to access the unconscious can start us on the path to de-condition our conditioning! If we have no means to access and re-program the mind, to assert our will, we lack the ability to control our own fate. Without knowing about the conscious and unconscious mind, we tend to misunderstand or lend mystical interpretations to natural occurrences—in other words, to be blind to our programming and to become products of our culture and society.

You might say, "Yes, I already know all this." Well then, do you consciously access and control your unconscious mind? Do you know how to find out what your programming is? Do you know how to stop random and unintentional programming from happening to you? Are you able to reach within and re-program the limitations that haunt you, to untangle those psychological complexes that are hidden underneath? Or instead, are you just a reflection of your culture and time? If you are *not* screening and changing your programming, you may be minimizing your free will.

Why Bother?

You might think, *I am not a reactive being. I am not programmed. I am an individual. I have my own ideas. I'm different from my culture and friends.*

But take a good look around you. Too many simply react to stimuli, chase what feels good and run from what feels bad. This governs most of their life decisions: food, shelter, security, pleasure and procreation.

In reality, our surface-level feelings and conscious awareness are the least of what we are. However, too many think that this is what is important. There is so much more that happens behind the scenes in our minds, in our unconscious, that affects us. It is the I behind the scenes that calls the shots and truly drives our lives.

My point is that what occurs in your unconscious mind is extremely relevant to your life, to who you are and to what you are doing in life. The way your life looks right now, whether it is the life you've always dreamed of living or the one you are forced to live, it is largely the result of your unconscious mind. The human mind can be either our greatest asset or our greatest enemy. As Marcus Aurelius said, "Happiness depends on the quality of your thoughts!"[120]

When our mind is running amok, it brings us to the depth of despair; when expectations are too low, it leads to a mediocre life likely to miss its true potential. At its zenith, the mind helps us achieve our ultimate aspiration: Happiness, lasting and stable, which is grounded in our own self-sufficiency.

A New Understanding

Without the conscious mind's ability to access the unconscious, we would not be much different from other animals. There is nothing wrong with other animals, but animals are instinct-driven creatures. Instinct is simply more powerful programming. An animal can only be what it was born to be, what its instincts dictate, with very limited variation. Humanity has a special asset: the ability to consciously access our unconscious depths and override our instinctual behavior. Without this, free will is impossible.

If an animal has a good environment, it is happy; if it is in a bad environment, it suffers. Mentally, humans have the ability to change our frame of reference. Animals generally do not. Therefore, humans—unlike animals—have the ability to control how they react to stress and suffering. Do not underestimate this extremely helpful asset. It is extremely helpful. Granted, most people do not yet know they possess this skill, and this is what this book is about.

Part of our new understanding is realizing that our greatest asset is to be able to reach within the unconscious, affect our fate, activate our free will and move beyond Self-Actualization. Access to the unconscious gives us inspiration and direction, releases us from the stresses and sufferings of life, and gives us the ability to purify the programming that causes negativities.

Most ancient cultures believed that inspiration was aided by God(s) or supernatural entities. We now know that the unconscious is a storage bank of information and a gateway to powerful and untapped abilities. Our inspirations— inventions, art and music–were once emotions, feelings and impulses, hidden within these unconscious depths. In *The Creative Brain: The Science of Genius*, Nancy Andreasen shows that it is the unconscious mind that is the seat of inspiration.[121] Some might say that the unconscious is inspired by God or by an intelligent Universe. This is an assumption, but whatever the truth might be, does it not behoove us to learn how to reach within and unlock our latent abilities? At the least, why not learn to calm the mind, reduce stress and achieve Inner-Actualization?

You might be saying to yourself, "My life is great. I am inspired all the time, and I access the unconscious randomly when I dream."

Even when we are fortunate enough to have a life that is mostly stress-free, there are no guarantees that this won't change. Rather than random access, why not access our highest potentials purposefully? Overcome your limitations. Attain true freedom. When we are freed from the constraining influence of our instinctual reactions, our conscious mind is able to more effectively direct our responses to instincts and external stimuli.

Our Programming

Am I programmed? Impulses and instincts are examples of our auto reactions. Behavior done without mindfulness, (i.e. without the input of the conscious will), is a product of mental programing. Some instincts are hard-wired others changeable.

Are you currently able to monitor your programming, your impulses and reactions, on a conscious level? If you are aware of and able to control your negative unconscious reactions and programming, then you are also able to exercise free will. If, on the other hand you are not aware or not in control of your reactions—then *your programming is running you.* It is the external environment that is your true master, not your higher mind. Other people and influences are running your life whether you realize it or not. Your programming is overriding your conscious mind, intellectual decisions and free will. You are then a slave to forces below the threshold of consciousness. We do not have much room for free will, unless we are able to interject conscious choice and awareness into what is otherwise unconscious and take hold of our free will.

Consequences of our Programming

The consequence of our negative programming is unnecessary suffering. An example of how we use our minds incorrectly and thus of how we unnecessarily experience stress is when we create the state of boredom within the mind. Boredom is weak thinking. It is unnecessary suffering. When we are bored, we are not satisfied with what exists in this current moment. We dislike reality as it is. We imagine another reality and suffer because we do not have what we imagine. We are wishing for something other than what we are experiencing, and this causes us stress and inner pain. In a situation where nothing bad is happening, it is not reality that is bad. It is our perception of reality that is causing us to suffer. When we are bored, we are focused on suffering, rather than seeing the happiness within. Change your perception of the moment, and this will change your reality.

Every moment can be wonderful when one is perceiving reality correctly, when we are experiencing the fullness of being. Incorrect ways of thinking can be changed. We can make the mind function differently, so that it does not get bored, so that it does not experience stress unnecessarily. Pain is unavoidable, but suffering does not need to exist. It is created by our mind, by our thinking. It is thus the result of a mind that we have not trained properly.

Your Current Reactions

How do you currently react to your psychological stress? Do you allow it to become suffering? How do you currently alleviate your stress and inner pain?

Diversions sometimes seem to alleviate stress, but more often, they tend to create or prolong suffering. How? They pacify the inner pain, so it seems that they have solved a problem. But instead, they cause a new problem: often, we become attached to our diversions. We then have the original suffering along with a perceived need for the diversion. What this looks like is:

1. We feel stress and suffering.
2. We engage in some sort of external activity to divert our attention.
3. The diversion becomes our focus, so we become temporarily distracted.
4. Then the cycle repeats, and the diversion often becomes a source of attachment, a golden chain.

Suffering is Not Our Friend

"Pain is inevitable, suffering is optional."
—HARUKI MURAKAMI.

Some people reading this might be so rooted in their suffering and cycles of action and reaction that they may wonder why I even bring these things up. It may seem to some that our reactions, diversions, suffering and programming are the natural order of things—that there is no way to escape, as if stress and suffering were unavoidable. Even though it hurts them, some actually like suffering and believe that suffering is advantageous.

None of these things are true. We can learn and live without stress and suffering. People free themselves from their suffering every day, and they have for thousands of years. They lead better lives as a result. All that is required is a different process of thinking.

Ever notice that some people attract difficulty? They call suffering into their lives both consciously and unconsciously. They say they want a stress-free life—*but they call forth the opposite*.

When I say this, I am not judging anyone. We are all valuable. We are all equally searching to be happy and doing the best we know how. Besides, we are not our actions. I am referring to unnecessary reactions. They are...well, *unnecessary*. The point is to operate in such a way as to produce the best results. Unfortunately, some people suffer and do nothing about it. Not knowing that there is a different way of being, they revel in their programming. They actually believe that they cannot grow without suffering.

An Example of My Unnecessary Suffering

I too was an adherent of this type of negative programming until I discovered my error at a twenty-day vipassana meditation course. During such courses, one is "stuck" in a meditation facility with nothing else to do but meditate—all day, every day, for days on end. This is helpful because it cuts away all distractions. Unless an emergency arises, a staple part of the course is that you do not communicate with anyone, read, write, or watch TV. Your only responsibility is to meditate—that is, you are simply present with your inner self. The idea is to focus within. Normally, we do not get this opportunity in everyday life but find ourselves motivated to focus externally. One of the outcomes of an intense meditation regimen is that eventually you come to observe what the mind is doing, without distractions.

What was my mind doing? Before I re-programmed this particular conditioning, rather than being at peace, my mind went out of its way to suffer! It did everything possible to think thoughts that would make me suffer. Can you believe it? My mind felt it necessary to suffer! For the longest time, I felt that a course was not a course unless I suffered—no pain, no gain. That was my programming.

I was in a place where all my needs were met. I had great food and shelter. The facilities and environment of the course were superb. There were no other people to cause my problems. All my needs were fulfilled. I had no reason to feel stress. All I had to do was be happy. Yet instead, I chose to suffer. This was an awakening for me. I asked myself, "Why? Why am I choosing to suffer? Why not just be happy!?"

I realized that in my own life, my suffering was occurring

because of my thoughts, not because of anything external. Yes, I know that you might say that external events make life easier or more difficult. This is true. However, we do not have to suffer unnecessarily.

When I was revolving in my cycle of suffering, I blamed other people for my stress, or I blamed external events. I was unconsciously inviting difficulty into my life, rather than reveling in the peace that can be found in every moment. I glorified my difficulties and defined myself by them. This is a victim's mentality, and it creates a self-perpetuating cycle. During these meditation courses, I came to realize that stress was optional, even if at times external events brought pain. I had stop contributing to my own suffering.

This makes me think of all the people I know who are waiting for life to be perfect and thus, they hope, free of catalysts for stress. As a rule, life will not be exactly like we want it to be. It usually produces some event or other that we do not want. Our only hope is to change our programming and learn not to suffer in the face of such pain.

Secular Principles

Freeing the mind from inner pain is easier said than done. Realizing that we do not want to suffer is merely half the battle. The other half is to learn how to access and to re-program the mind's negative patterns. Let us assume that we truly realize, on a conscious level, that suffering is optional. What then? Why do we still suffer, and how can we stop?

To exercise our free will, it is imperative to access the unconscious mind. Being able to control our mind allows us to attain our goals. I find that the following principles make life better.

1. **Purposefully access the unconscious mind** daily and regularly; practice a secular meditation technique that frees you of your limitations and produces inner peace and Inner-Actualization. In other words, eradicate negative reactive patterns in the Lower Unconscious, trust your Higher Unconscious Mind and learn to differentiate between the two.

   Without this, moving beyond the emptiness is quite difficult. Rather than trying to avoid the unpleasant and becoming attached to pleasant thoughts, things and activities, learn to be happy with each moment as it is, from within—and you will not suffer when external things change or become disappointing. Life will then be concerned with more than mere survival, the constant acquisition of pleasure, things, goals, or the striving for Safety, Social and Esteem Needs. Knowing this intellectually is

only the first step to practicing this on an unconscious level through training in meditation.

2. **Continuously remind yourself to be happy, at peace, in the moment**; it is you and not events that make you happy or unhappy. All your moments added together make up your life. What you say to yourself and to others about the circumstances you subject yourself to in life are important, since they either program you to be satisfied or to suffer either lock you within the realm of Self-Actualization or help take you beyond.

3. **Refrain from harm and instead do good**. Keep your thoughts and actions positive. What you put out into the world comes back to you in some way, sooner or later. Our thoughts become our actions, and our actions become our fate. This too must be enacted first on an unconscious level. Train your mind on an unconscious level to help others, to be truthful, to be mindful, to love, and to do no harm to yourself or to other beings.

4. **Help other beings**. The ultimate way to help someone is to help them achieve inner peace or Inner-Actualization.

5. **Seek and then represent the truth**. Go within and access unconscious information, then test your assumptions by using critical thinking, reason and

analysis. Let go of dogma. Do not mistake opinions
for facts.

These items represent the Secular Buddhist principles
of right conduct, wisdom and meditation (*sila, samadhi,
panna*). They are the basis of a secular, psychological, form
of spirituality, which requires no need for religion, belief
in God(s), gurus, or supernaturalism. I find that when one
lives in opposition to these principles, or if any of them are
missing from one's life, then life becomes more difficult for
self or others.

Purposeful Mindfulness Intentional and self-controlled trance state that uses methods such as meditation to allow access to the processes of the unconscious mind, giving the ability to program or re-program limitations and to use Internal Sources.

Spontaneous Mindfulness Trance state that is undirected or uncontrolled.

Chapter 12

An Outward Journey Leading Within

"When a thing is new, people say, 'It is not true'. Later, when its truth becomes obvious, they say, 'It is not important.' Finally, when its importance cannot be denied, they say, 'Anyway, it is not new.'"—WILLIAM JAMES.

Best News of All

Imagine walking down a beautiful beach. The sun is shining. The water is a crystalline blue, glints in the sun. Birds arch in the sky; others run down the beach beside you, darting left, darting right, catching food.

The next thing you know, you are looking at a magic lamp in the sand. It is of amazing workmanship, hand-crafted and studded with precious stones. As is usual in these stories, you pick up the lamp and rub it, and a genie comes out. Wearing flowing robes and enigmatic smile, she offers to grant you one of two wishes. *Wish one is life-changing, wish two mind-changing.*

If she grants you the first wish, you will immediately receive enough money so that you will never have to work again. You will therefore be able to obtain anything external that you want. You will have enough money to help yourself, your friends, family and anyone else you meet with any material desire they should have. With your material needs fulfilled, you will instantly become financially secure, joining the wealthiest one percent of the world's population.

There are a few catches, however. Catch number one is that as you enjoy your wealth, you will notice that you are dependent on it for your happiness. So when you are not doing something external, you are suffering inside. Two, you will notice that even though you're now wealthy, you are still subject to suffering, life's changing nature, death and disease. Three, your life and resources are bountiful right now, but they are limited and subject to change. You were given great wealth, but that wealth requires upkeep. Adverse situations in life may strip you of your wealth. Four, you are still mortal, and upon your death you will lose everything that you love and depend on for your happiness.

Now the other choice: if she grants you the second wish, your life will not change externally. Everything you have that is material or external will remain exactly as it was before you met the genie. You will have the same financial and social position. The gift you will receive from the genie will be a mental skill. You will learn how to be at peace with the stress and suffering that are an inevitable part of life. Thereafter, you will be satisfied with every one of life's moments, no matter what the moments bring.

Yes, you will still enjoy life, find beauty in it, love and achieve your goals. However, now, you will no longer suffer. Your craving for that which you do not have will go away. Therefore, events will just be. This state of mind does not forbid the use of wealth or luxury, but it is not required for your happiness. This is because your happiness will no longer be based on the external things that change. Therefore, bad things and bad situations will occur; there will be reasons to experience stress, but you will not be hurt by them. Life may or may not favor you materially. You will, though, have internal happiness.

No matter what your external circumstances or what becomes of you in this life or even the next, if there exists such a thing, you will be free of suffering. As in the first scenario, in this one too you will be able to share this gift with others. Along with this skill-set, you will have the ability to teach others to think the same way. You will be able to share this with whomever you wish, so they too cease to suffer if they are wise enough to choose this gift.

Which of these two genie gifts would you take? Which gift is better for you and your loved ones? We can achieve what we want, according to our utmost capabilities. *Choose your wants carefully.* Then, access the unconscious mind.

In reality, we do get both wishes, daily, and we can experience them at the same time. Unfortunately, most people just settle for one, the external form of happiness, and then they suffer.

My Personal Experience with Inner-Actualization

The meditation center in Jaipur seemed so peaceful, like heaven on earth; but it was my mind that was now at peace. After meditating for hours on end, for days on end, grappling with the mind, with my past, my conscience, and negative habit patterns that assailed me, and I finally reached a plateau. Plateaus occur all the time. They are in no way the ultimate end to the work. They should not be sought as a means to an end. However, it was during the time I spent on one of these plateaus that I realized that I was truly satisfied. Satisfaction and peace of mind came from within, and I did not need anything external to experience it. I had found an inner source that I could take with me. It was a sense of ultimate peace. I saw the perfection in each separate moment. All was perfect, just as it was. I needed nothing else.

This, for me, was a revelation. Until then, I had always tried to divert my attention from each moment. I did not know how to be happy with reality as it was. Inner-Actualization worked. For months after that experience, from time to time, I flourished in this newfound state of mind. I did everyday things and perceived all as perfect. I now had a tool that allowed me to learn to enjoy each moment and to not suffer unnecessarily, no matter what happened to me in life. With Inner-Actualization, I would always be okay. Inner-Actualization is not just about happiness and peace, for this can come in many forms. It is about peace and happiness that come from deep within and don't depend on external circumstances.

I thought about all my friends and loved ones who have never experienced such a feeling. They were busy chasing money, careers, titles, education, sex, drugs and countless other diversions in an effort to gain this sort of satisfaction. Yet none of these external preoccupations could ever produce such a state.

The Greatest Good

"Watch your thoughts, they become your words.
Watch your words, they become your actions.
Watch your actions, they become your habits.
Watch your habits, they become your character.
Watch your character, it becomes your destiny."
—MAHATMA GANDHI

It is easy enough to say, "Be mindful and happy in the moment." Inner peace is here, right now, for everyone. But to experience this state, moment-to-moment, every moment, is another matter. This requires an in-depth practice of meditation, a restructuring of the mind. The mind needs to be retrained to see things from a different perspective. We need to change the way our unconscious processes information. Then we can go on about our lives and do all the things we usually do, Inner-Actualized. This takes time, effort, and a meditation technique that will access the unconscious. Until that method is perfected and you learn to *be* in the moment, chances are the mind will continue to suffer.

Sometimes, the problem seems so innocent. I hear it a lot, from all kinds of people: "I am a talker...I have to keep moving...I have to do something...I cannot sit still...I get bored easily." Why is it that we are so driven to keep talking, moving and doing nonstop?

We do not always feel good, and life does not always produce the results that we want. The challenge is that we need to do mundane things to survive, and at the same time we yearn to attain a state of non-suffering and satisfaction. But then we become caught up in surviving and solving the everyday problems and often lose track of the ultimate goal. One impulse initiates the next set of impulses, and this forms reaction cycles that take over our intentions and free will. When the mind is conditioned to suffer, it hurts to be still; in the stillness, we feel our pain. Our inner suffering does not allow us to be in the here-and-now, to experience the wonder around us, to be happy with what is, with this moment. For the untrained mind, *being* hurts; it is stressful. Thus to stop the suffering, we do everything possible— including harming ourselves and others—to be distracted *from ourselves. Moving, talking and doing keep us distracted from our inner psychology.*

We strive for the best in ourselves, we champion happiness, ethical behavior, goodwill and personal growth, and then we find ourselves unable to follow the ideals we have set for ourselves when our mental reactions sabotage our best intentions. As the Buddha said:

> No one can harm you as much as you can be harmed by your own unruly mind. To defeat armies and nations and to vanquish thousands of men in battle is not as great or profitable as to gain control over one's own mind. Our greatest enemy in the world, and our greatest friend in the world, is often our own mind.[61]

Oddly, sadly, suffering due to one's own mind is normal, even if unnecessary. Since so many people experience this cycle of suffering and diversion, most think this is unavoidable. People might even be insulted if you were to point this out to them. Perhaps this is just our ego that stops us from learning to re-train the mind? This is an age-old problem; the ancients too had their excuses. Ancient people who were unfamiliar with science and had no other way to explain mental phenomena often turned to supernatural explanations. They personified their minds' unwanted reactions as coming from separate beings, evil forces and devils. Personifying unexplained phenomena gives an explanation, but it can also rob us of our ability to know the true cause of the problem, and it also places the solution outside ourselves. This is a natural reaction. Humanity has done this in all cultures and in all times and geographies. Just look at the multitudes of supernatural beings we have believed in throughout the centuries. Blaming our misdeeds, inabilities and mental ineptitudes on a devil or on fate can be a way to avoid taking personal responsibility.

It is entirely possible that our purpose in this life is to achieve our greatest potential—to finally become satisfied and go beyond Self-Actualization. This greatest good is fueled from within; it belongs to you and helps you attain inner peace.

As Jung taught, the message of the unconscious is of greater importance than most people realize. As consciousness is exposed to all sorts of external attractions and distractions, it is easily led astray and seduced into following ways that do nothing to promote peace.

George Grimm said it very well, "We are sick, we suffer from the disease of the willing. [t]his disease is chronic: we have suffered from it all through beginning-less time."[122] The medicine, the cure, is the insight of meditation. "In contrast to its merely symptomatic treatment by the ordinary person—who only temporarily soothes the incipient strings of desires by yielding to them, with the result that the disease only grows worse."[122]

The world brings lovely surprises and at the same time threatening dark clouds, heart-wrenching pain and an endless palette of sorrows. We have a choice—wallow in the mud of pleasant dreams, forever chasing Externals that do not satisfy, or go within and learn to meditate. Quench the fire as soon as possible. Time is short. If you wait, the opportunity may slip away, and the world may suck you back in to its warm delirium of empty promises.

The solution is to achieve the greatest good by changing the unconscious programming that can limit us, but the work starts within, and it is this work that is the highest heroic act. If, after survival, Inner-Actualization is the ultimate goal, then why not help people nurture the ability to access the unconscious and achieve inner peace? Then, we will have a ready-made internal source of power, no matter what we encounter in life. This is the greatest possible way to help others and to help ourselves.

This is why secular meditation is not only the most important tool for us, but also for our loved ones. Purposeful meditation gives us ready-made balance, from within; it can remind us that we are worthy and loved, whether there is an external reason to feel this way or not. An internal locus of control gives us comfort, confidence and the power to achieve our greatest dreams. Painful and unwanted events will continue to happen, but suffering will be lessened.

If you have children, it is your duty to do what is best for them physically and psychologically. As far as I know, there is nothing nobler than empowering a person's inner transformation. The greatest gift you can give a loved one is peace of mind that provides them a bulwark against life's pitfalls. Everything external that you give to yourself or others is likely outside of your control, subject to death or decay.

I suspect that many modern readers are results-oriented, like I am, and want a solution that contains the essence an essential truth or a "cure," without any fluff. Religious and supernatural answers, on the other hand, seem to me to be mostly a fancy box, jammed with centuries of "packing material" and the "wrappings" of the outside world. The pearls of wisdom within get lost in the packaging.

My hope is that reading this book has given you an opportunity to reflect on your life. You now know about Inner-Actualization, the power of the unconscious mind, and about Internal and External Sources of happiness, and you know that it is possible to produce wonderment and equanimity from within. If your other needs have been met and you are able to pursue Inner-Actualization, then continue to meditate ceaselessly.

Take long meditation courses, join a weekly meditation group and help inspire others. But, if you still need to achieve the external needs, daily activities will likely try to get in the way of you meditating regularly. Here too, a weekly meditation group will offer support, and a ten-day mindfulness meditation retreat is one of the best ways to learn to meditate. At the retreat, your basic needs will be met, and you will be able to concentrate on the inner path without distractions. Secular meditation courses are also offered for children, so your entire family can benefit. Learn secular meditation. The opportunity to systematically ponder your otherwise unconscious reactions is a rare gift. It is the key to understanding your existence.

If you already have the necessary mind tools and a direction in life, I do not want to discourage you. Continue to practice it if it alleviates your suffering. But, if you still experience suffering, then explore further your ability to access the unconscious and change your programming. Visit a secular meditation center and learn to meditate—learn to use Internal Sources. Contact me through my blog or website for more information: www.ExploringYourLife.com.

Find meaning in life
Help others
Attain inner peace,
Without
God (s), gurus, or
Supernaturalism

References

1. *Cyber-survivalists Planning For A Post-y2k Apocalypse.* **Brandon, Karen.** August 03, 1998, Chicago Tribune.
2. **Campbell, Joseph and Moyers, Bill.** *The Power of Myth.* s.l.: Anchor Books, a division of Random House, Inc., 1988. pp. xiii, 160, 231.
3. **Taren, Adrienne, et al.** *Dispositional Mindfulness Co-Varies with Smaller Amygdala and Caudate Volumes in Community Adults.* PLOS DOI: 10.1371/journal.pone.0064574. [Online]. 2013, 22-May [Cited: 2013, 29-August.] http://www.plosone.org/article/info:doi/10.1371/journal.pone.0064574.
4. **Stoye, John.** *The Siege of Vienna: The Last Great Trial Between Cross & Crescent.* New York: Pegasus Books, 2007.
5. *"John III Sobieski." The World Book Encyclopedia.* Volume 1. Chicago: World Book, Inc., 2007. p. 132. 0-7166-0107-9.
6. **Dawisha, Karen and Parrott, Bruce, [ed.].** *The Consolidation of Democracy in East-Central Europe (Democratization and Authoritarianism in Post-Communist Societies).* Cambridge: Cambridge University Press, 1997. p. 71. 978-0521599382.
7. **Petrovic, Ivana and Miller, John F.** *"Apollo." The Oxford Encyclopedia of Ancient Greece and Rome.* [ed.] Michael Gagarin. s.l.: Oxford University Press. The Oxford Encyclopedia of Ancient Greece and Rome: (e-reference edition), 2010.
8. *"Motivation." Encyclopædia Britannica Online Library Edition.* s.l.: Encyclopædia Britannica, Inc., 2012.
9. **Maslow, A. H.** *A Theory of Human Motivation.* s.l.: Psychological Review, 1943. pp. 370-396. Vol. 50.
10. **Hannay, Alastair.** *Kierkegaard: A Biography.* Cambridge: Cambridge University Press, 2003. 0521513810.
11. "Philip K. Dick". *www.answers.com.* [Online] 2012. [Cited: 2012, 7-July.] http://www.answers.com/topic/philip-k-dick.
12. **Thoreau, Henry David and Miller, Scot.** *Walden: 150th Anniversary Illustrated Edition of the American Classic.* New York: Hoghton Mifflin Company, 2004. pp. 27, 127.

13. *"Sisyphus."* Encyclopædia Britannica Online Library Edition. s.l.: Encyclopædia Britannica, Inc., 2012.

14. *"What is psychodynamics?"* WebMD, Stedman's Medical Dictionary 28th Edition. s.l.: Lippincott Williams & Wilkins, 2006.

15. **Millon, Theodore, Grossman, Seth and Meagher, Sarah E.** *Masters of the Mind: Exploring the Story of Mental Illness from Ancient Times to the New Millennium.* Hoboken: John Wiley & sons, Inc., 2002. pp. 5, 6, 15, 25, 26. 0-471-46985-8.

16. **Roccatagliata, Giuseppe.** *A History of Ancient Psychiatry (Contributions in Medical Studies).* s.l.: Greenwood Press, 1986. 8-0313244193.

17. *"Byzantine Empire."* Encyclopædia Britannica Online Library Edition. Web: s.n. pp. 1, 43.

18. *"Roman Empire."* Encyclopædia Britannica Online Library Edition. Web: Encyclopædia Britannica, Inc., s.n., 2012. p. 2.

19. **Ellerbe, Helen.** *The Dark Side of Christian History.* San Rafael: Morningstar Books, 1995.

20. *"psychology."* Encyclopædia Britannica Online Library Edition. Web: Encyclopædia Britannica, Inc., 2012. pp. 2, 5, 194.

21. **Shapero, Hannah M.G.** Zoroastrianism, Judaism, and Christianity. *Pyracantha.* [Online] 1997, 6-September. [Cited: 2012, 3-February.] http://www.pyracantha.com/Z/zjc3.html.

22. **Stark, Rodney.** *The Victory of Reason: How Christianity Led to Freedom, Capitalism, and Western Success.* New York: Random House, 2005.

23. **Maddison, Angus.** *Contours of the World Economy 1-2030 AD: Essays in Macro-Economic History.* Oxford: Oxford University Press, 2007. pp. 4-7.

24. **Haggard, Howard W.** *The Doctor in History.* New York: Barnes & Noble, Inc., 1962. p. 164.

25. **Bonanos, Christopher.** *Gods, Heroes and Philosophers: a celebration of all things greek.* s.l.: Citadel Press Books, 2005.

26. **Scaglia, Beatriz.** *Those Who Establish Greatness: The Founding Fathers and Mothers of Medicine and Physiology.* London: Websters Digital Services, 2011. p. 426.

27. **Bynum, W. F., Browne, E. J. and Porter, Roy.** *The Macmillan Dictionary of the History of Science.* London: MacMillan, 1981. p. 292.

28. *"Freud, Sigmund." Encyclopædia Britannica Online Library Edition.* Web: Encyclopædia Britannica, Inc., 2012.

29. *"Jung, Carl." Encyclopædia Britannica Online Library Edition.* Web: Encyclopædia Britannica, Inc., 2012.

30. **Storr, Anthony.** *The Essential Jung.* New Jersey: Princeton University Press, 1983. pp. 18, 19, 79, 182-200. 0-691-02935-0.

31. **Allison, Nancy.** *The Illustrated Encyclopedia of Body-Mind Disciplines.* New York: Rosen Publishing Group, 1999. p. 74.

32. *"Hypnosis." Encyclopædia Britannica Online Library Edition.* Web: Encyclopædia Britannica, Inc., 2012.

33. **Ni, Maoshing.** *The Yellow Emperor's Classic of Medicine: A New Translation of the Neijing Suwen with Commentary.* Boston: Shambala Publications, 1995. 978-0-8348-25765.

34. *"Pali Literature." Encyclopædia Britannica Online Library Edition.* Web: Encyclopædia Britannica, Inc., 2012.

35. **Ṭhānissaro, Bhikkhu.** *Noble Strategy: Essays on the Buddhist Path.* Valley Center: Meta Forest Monastery, 1999. The Healing Power of the Precepts.

36. **Johnston, William M.** *Encyclopedia of Monasticism: M-Z.* Chicago: Fitzroy Dearborn Publishers, 2000. p. 186.

37. **Thera, Narada.** *Buddhism in a Nutshell.* The Wheel Publications Special Issue. Kandy: Buddhist Publication Society, 1975. Chapter 9.

38. **Thera, Soma.** *Kalama Sutta: The Buddha's Charter of Free Inquiry: The Wheel Publication No. 8.* Kandy: Buddhist Publication Society, 1987.

39. **Nyanaponika, Thera.** *The Vision of Dhamma: Buddhist Writings of Nyanaponika Thera.* Kandy: Buddhist Publication Society, 1994. pp. 292-295.

40. **Ajahn Chah, Venerable.** *Living Dhamma.* Wat Pah Nanachat: The Sangha, 1992.

41. **Thanissaro, Bhikkhu.** *The Paradox of Becoming.* s.l.: Thanissaro Bhikkhu, 2008.

42. **Bullen, Leonard A.** *Buddhism A Method of Mind -Training. Bodhi Leaves No. B42.* Kandy: Buddhist Publication Society, 1969.

43. **Bodhi, Bhikkhu.** *The Noble Eightfold Path: Way to the End of Suffering.* Onalaska: Pariyatti Publishing, 2006. 978-1928706076.

44. *"Mysticism." Encyclopædia Britannica Online Library Edition.* 2012: Encyclopædia Britannica, Inc., Web.

45. **Nyanaponika, Thera.** *Five Mental Hindrances.* Kandy: Buddhist Publication Society, 1998. 978-9552401114.

46. **Yapko, Michael D.** *Mindfulness and Hypnosis: The Power of Suggestion to Transform Experience.* Faifield: W. W. Norton & Company, 2011. p. 122.

47. **Tallis, Frank.** *Hidden Minds: A History of the Unconscious.* New York: Arcade Publishing, 2002. 978-1-61145-505-2.

48. **Keeney, Bradford PhD and Erickson, Betty Alice MS, [ed.].** *Milton H. Erickson, M.D.: An American Healer (Profiles in Healing series).* s.l.: Leete's Island Books, 2006. 978-0918172556.

49. **Fromm, Erika and Shor, Ronald E.** *Hypnosis: Research Developments And Perspectives.* Piscataway: AldineTransaction, 2009. pp. 32-33.

50. **Donald, Robertson.** "Sigmund Freud." Experts Define Hypnosis. *UK Hypnosis.* [Online] 2002-2009. [Cited: 2012, 10-July.] http://www.ukhypnosis.com/Definitions.htm.

51. **Brann, Les, Owens, Jacky and Williamson, Ann, [ed.].** *The Handbook of Contemporary Clinical Hypnosis: Theory and Practice.* Chichester: John Wiley & Sons, Ltd., 2012. p. Chapter 3. 978-0-470-68367-5.

52. **Marshall, Sir John.** p. 44. *Mohenjo-daro.* 1922 and 1927. s.l.: Indological Book House, 1973.

53. **Marshall, John Hubert.** *Mohenjo-daro and the Indus civilization: Being an official account of archaeological excavations at Mohenjo-daro carried out by the Government of India between the years 1922 and 1927.* s.l.: Indological Book House, 1973. p. 106.

54. **Goenka, S.N. and Confalonieri, Pierluigi.** *The Clock of Vipassana has Struck:A Tribute to The Saintly Life and Legacy of a Lay Master of Vipassana Meditation (The Teachings and Writings of Sayagyi U Ba Khin).* Seattle: Vipassana Research Publications, 1999. pp. 84, 68, 72.

55. **Jung, C.G.** *The Undiscovered Self: With Symbols and the Interpretation of Dreams.* [trans.] R. F. C. Hull. New Jersey: Princeton University Press, 1990. p. 5:491. 978-0-691-15051-2.

56. **Magazine, Bound.** *STUDIA LITURGICA: An International*

Ecumenical Quarterly for Liturgical Research and Renewal. 1972: s.n. Vol. 9.

57. **Erickson, Milton H. and Rosen, Sidney.** *My Voice Will Go With You: The Teaching Tales of Milton H. Erickson, M.D.* New York: W. W. Norton & Company, Ltd., 1982. pp. 19, 113. 978-0393301359.

58. **Erickson, Milton H. and Rossi, Ernest L.** *Hypnotherapy: An Exploratory Casebook.* s.l.: Irvington Pub; Har/Cas edition, 1980. p. 18. 978-0829002447.

59. **Milton, H. Erickson, Rossi, Ernest L. and Rossi, Sheila I.** *Hypnotic Realities: The Induction of Clinical Hypnosis and Forms of Indirect Suggestion.* s.l.: John Wiley & Sons, Inc., 1977. p. Forward. 978-0470151693.

60. **Thanissaro, Bhikkhu.** Saṃyutta Nikāya: Magga Saṃyutta: Avijja Sutta: Ignorance. *Free Dharma.* [Online] Canonical, 2000. [Cited: 2012, 10-July.] http://www.freedharma.com/text/canonical/anna-tra_sutta/ed1f0fd27b04d370d130aeab92b09fe7//index.shtml.

61. **Thera, Narada, [trans.].** *The Dhammapada.* Colombo: B.M.S. Publications, 1978. p. 35.

62. **Bodhi, Bhikkhu, [trans.].** *The Connected Discourses of the Buddha: A Translation of the Samyutta Nikaya.* Somerville: Wisdom Publications, 2000. pp. 1263-1265. 0-86171-331-1.

63. **Mlodinow, Leonard.** *Subliminal: How Your Unconscious Mind Rules Your Behavior.* New York: Pantheon Books, 2012. pp. 33, 52-78, 62, 91, 96, 197-220. 978-0307378217.

64. **Packard, Vance.** *The Hidden Persuaders.* Brooklyn: Ig Publishing, 2007.

65. **Lindstrom, Martin.** *Brandwashed: Tricks Companies Use to Manipulate Our Minds and Persuade Us to Buy.* New York: Crown Publishing Group, 2011. p. 12.

66. **Willock, Brent, Bohm, Lori C. and Curtis, Rebecca C.** *Taboo or not Taboo? Forbidden Thoughts, Forbidden Acts in Psychoanalysis and Psychotherapy (Developments in Psychoanalysis).* London: Karnac Books, Ltd., 2009. p. 7.

67. **Freud, Sigmund and Strachey, James.** *On Metapsychology: Theory of Psychoanalysis: Beyond the Pleasure Principle, Ego*

and the Id and Other Works. s.l.: Penguin Books, Ltd., 1984. 978-0140217407.

68. **Freud, Sigmund.** *The Ego and the Id.* s.l.: Pacific Publishing Studio, 2010. 978-1451537239.

69. *"Mind." Dictionary.com Unabridged.* Web: Random House, Inc., 2012.

70. **Vilord, Thomas J.** *1001 Motivational Quotes for Success.* Cherry Hill: Garden State Publishing, 2002.

71. **Jeffrey, SB.** *An Introduction To Buddhist Philosophy From Metaphysics to Nirvana.* s.l.: Webster's Digital Services, 2011. p. 93.

72. *Siegfried and Roy Vegas marquee removed.* [online] s.l.: United Press International, Inc., 2004.

73. **Nash, Alan.** Siegfried and Roy: The Night of the Tiger Attack. *Reader's Digest.* 2004.

74. *Eastern Wisdom Modern Life: Collected Talks, 1960-1969.* Novato: New World Library, 1994, 1995, 1996, 2008. 978-1-57731-180-5.

75. **Gabbard, Glen O., Litowitz, Bonnie E. and Williams, Paul, [ed.].** *Textbook of Psychoanalysis.* Arlington: American Psychiatric Publishing, Inc., 2012. pp. 13-14, 94, 96, 159, 178, 572.

76. **Collins, Steven.** *Selfless Persons: Imagery and Thought in Theravada Buddhism.* Cambridge: Cambridge University Press, 1982.

77. **Perez-Ramon, Joacquin.** *Self & Non-Self in Early Buddhism.* s.l.: Mouton De Gruyter, 1980.

78. **Campbell, Joseph.** *The Masks of God: Oriental mythology.* New York: Penguin Group, 1962.

79. **Mahathera, Nyantiloka, et al.** *The Three Basic Facts of Existence: Egolessness.* Kandy: Buddhist Publication Society, 1973. Vol. III Nos. 202/203/204.

80. **Burnham, Alex.** *Freud's Psychic Apparatus Through Dr. Seuss.* Norderstedt: GRIN Verlag, 2011.

81. *"Superego." Encyclopædia Britannica Online Library Edition.* Web: Encyclopædia Britannica, Inc., 2012.

82. *"Ego, superego, and id".* [Online] s.l.: New World Encyclopedia, 2006.

83. **de Berg, Henk.** *Freud's Theory and Its Use in Literary and Cultural Studies: An Introduction (Studies in German Literature, Linguistics, and Culture).* Rochester: Camden House, 2004. 1-57113-301-4.

84. *"Persona." Encyclopædia Britannica Online Library Edition.* Web: Encyclopædia Britannica, Inc., 2012.

85. *"Id, ego and super-ego."* [Online] s.l.: Wikimedia Foundation, Inc., 2012.

86. **Freud, Ann.** *The Ego and the Mechanisms of Defence: The Writings of Anna Freud.* London: Karnac Books, 1993. 85575-038-4.

87. **Cramer, Phebe PhD.** *Protecting the Self: Defense Mechanisms in Action.* New York: Guilford Press, 2006. 978-1593852986.

88. **Bodhi, Bhikkhu.** Anicca Vata Sankhara. *Access to Insight.* [Online] 2011, 16-June. [Cited: 2012, 5-September.] http://www.accesstoinsight.org/lib/authors/bodhi/bps-essay_43.html.

89. **Dawkins, Richard.** *River Out Of Eden: A Darwinian View Of Life (Science Masters Series).* New York: Basic Books, 1995. p. 6. 978-0465069903.

90. World POPClock Projection. *U.S. Census Bureau.* [Online] The United States Census Bureau, 2012, 18-September. [Cited: 2012, 18-September.] http://www.census.gov/main/www/popclock.html.

91. World Population. *Worldmeters.* [Online] 2012, 18-September. [Cited: 2012, 18-September.] http://www.worldometers.info/world-population/.

92. **Mulert, Christoph and Lemieux, Louis, [ed.].** *EEG - fMRI: Physiological Basis, Technique, and Applications.* s.l.: Springer-Verlag Berlin Heidelberg, 2010. 978-3540879183.

93. **Barlow, J.S.** *The Electroencephalogram: Its Patterns and Origins.* Massachusetts: massachusetts institute of technology. pp. 161, 165-166.

94. **Wolpaw, Jonathan and Wolpaw, Elizabeth Winter, [ed.].** *Brain-Computer Interfaces: Principles and Practice.* New York: Oxford University Press, 2012. 978-0195388855.

95. *"Positron Emission Tomography." Encyclopædia Britannica Online Library.* web: Encyclopædia Britannica, Inc., 2012.

96. *"Functional Magnetic Resonance Imaging." Encyclopædia Britannica Online.* Web: Encyclopædia Britannica, Inc., 2012.

97. **Ulmer, Stephan and Jansen, Olav, [ed.].** *fMRI: Basics and Clinical Applications.* s.l.: Springer-Verlag Berlin Heidelberg, 2009. 978-3540681311.

98. **Pert, Candice.** Your Body Is Your Subconscious Mind. *Your Body Is Your Subconscious Mind.* [Audiobook, CD, Audio CD] s.l.: Sounds True, Incorporated, 2004. 978-1591792239.

99. **Maclean, Paul D.** *The Triune Brain in Evolution: Role in Paleo-cerebral Functions.* New York: Plenum Press, 1990. pp. 8, 9. 978-0306431685.

100. **Strauss, Bob.** Prehistoric Crocodiles - The Ancient Cousins of the Dinosaurs; Everything You Ever Needed to Know About Crocodile Evolution. *www.about.com.* [Online] About.com a part of The New York Times Company, 2012, 13-September. http://dinosaurs.about.com/od/typesofdinosaurs/a/crocodilians.htm.

101. *"sexual behaviour, human."* Encyclopædia Britannica Online Library Edition. Web: Encyclopædia Britannica, Inc., 2012.

102. *"primate.".* Web: Encyclopædia Britannica, Inc., 2012.

103. **Caine, Renate Nummela and Caine, Geoffrey.** *Making Connections: Teaching and the Human Brain.* Nashville: Association for Supervision and Curriculum Development, 1990. p. 62. 978-0871201799.

104. The Triune Brain. *The Brain Compatible Project.* [Online] Buffalo State University of New York, 2012, 27-September. www.buffalostate.edu/orgs/bcp/brainbasics/triune.html.

105. The Triune Brain. *Wikipedia.* [Online] Wikimedia Foundation, Inc., 2012, 29-September. http://en.wikipedia.org/wiki/Triune_brain.

106. **Striedter, George F.** *Principles of Brain Evolution.* Sunderland: Sinauer Associates, 2005. 978-0878938209.

107. **Dabashi, Hamid.** *The Arab Spring: The End of Postcolonialism.* London: Zed Books, Ltd., 2012. 978-1780322247.

108. **Felton, R. Todd.** *Journey into the Transcendentalists' New England.* Berkeley: Roaring Forties Press, 2006. pp. 4-5. 978-0976670643.

109. **Richardson Jr., Robert D.** *Emerson: the mind on fire.* Berkeley and Los Angeles: University of California Press, 1995. p. 4. 978-0520088085.

110. **Jung, Carl Gustav.** *Man and His Symbols.* s.l.: Dell Publishing, 1968. p. 227. 978-0440351832.

111. **Jung, C.G.** *The Archetypes and The Collective Unconscious:*

Collected Works of C.G. Jung Vol.9 Part 1. [trans.] R.F.C. Hull.
New York: Bollingen Foundation, Inc., 1990. pp. 42-44.
978-0-691-01833-1.

112. **Bodhi, Bhikkhu.** *The Living Message of the Dhammapada.* Vol.
193. Kandy: Buddhist Publ. Society, 1993. pp. 42-43. Vol. Bodhi
Leaves No. 129.

113. **Pastorino, Ellen E. and Doyle-Portil, Susann M.** *What is Psychology?: Essentials.* 2. Belmont: Wadsworth Publishing, 2012. p.
123. 978-1111834159.

114. **Yapko, Michael D.** *Trancework: An Introduction to the Practice of Clinical Hypnosis.* 4. s.l.: Routledge, 2012. p. 54.
978-0415884945.

115. **Warren, Muriel Prince Dr.** *Trauma: Treatment and Transformation.* Lincoln: iUniverse, 2003.

116. **Copelan, Rachel.** *Hypnotism: Your Absoleute, Quintessntial, All
You Wanted to Know, Complete Guide.* Hollywood: Fredrick Fell
Publishers, Inc., 2000. p. 4.

117. *Investigation of Mindfulness Meditation Practitioners with Voxel-
based Morphometry.* **Hölzel, Britta K., et al.** Oxford: Oxford
University Press, 2008, March, Social Cognitive and Affective
Neuroscience, Vol. 3(1), pp. 55–61.

118. **Prophet, Elizabeth Clare.** *The Lost Years of Jesus: Documentary
Evidence of Jesus' 17-Year Journey to the East.* Gardiner: Summit
Publications, Inc., 1987. 978-0-916766870.

119. **Weir, Fred.** Russia emerges as Europe's most God-believ-
ing nation. *CS Monitor.* [Online] The Christian Science Monitor, 2011, 6-May. [Cited: 2012, 10-Oct.]
http://www.csmonitor.com/World/Europe/2011/0506/
Russia-emerges-as-Europe-s-most-God-believing-nation.

120. **Stokes, Philip.** *Philosophy: The World's Greatest Thinkers.* London: Arcturus Publishing Limited, 2012. p. 39.
978-1848378506.

121. **Andreasen, Nancy C.** *The Creative Brain: The Science of Genius.*
s.l.: Plume, 2006. 978-0452287815.

122. **Grimm, George.** *The Doctrine of the Buddha: The Religion of
Reason and Meditation.* [ed.] M. Keller-Grimm and Max Hoppe.
Delhi: Motilal Banarsidass, 1973. p. 356.

123. **Jung, Carl G.** *The Undiscovered Self.* s.l.: Signet, 2006. 978-0451217325.
124. **Hanson, Rick.** *How to Grow the Good in Your Brain.* Greater Good Science Center. [Online]. 2013, 23-September. [Cited: 2013, 27-October.] http://www.greatergood.berkeley.edu/article/item/how_to_grow_the_good_in_your_brain.
125. *"Marshall McLuhan." Encyclopædia Britannica Online Library Edition.* s.l.: Encyclopædia Britannica, Inc., 2012.
126. **Zeidan Fadel, et al.** *Brain Mechanisms Supporting the Modulation of Pain by Mindfulness Meditation.* The Journal of Neuroscience 31(14): 5540-5548; doi: 10.1523/JNEUROSCI.5791-10.2011. [Online]. 2011, 6-April [Cited: 2013, 1-December.] http://www.jneurosci.org/content/31/14/5540.long.
127. **Bodhi, Bhikkhu, [trans.].** *The Numerical Discourses of the Buddha: A Translation of the Anguttara Nikaya.* Somerville: Wisdom Publications, 2012. pp. 976-1-61429-044-5.
128. **Fleischman, Paul R.** *The Buddha Taught Nonviolence Not Pacifism.* Onalaska: Paryatti Press, 2002. p. 19. 978-1-928706-75-5.
129. *Uncovering the Codes for Reality.* **Tippet, Kristan.** s.l.: Krista Journal, 2012, Krista Journal, available at newsletter @onbeing.org.
130. **Osman, Ahmed.** http://dwij.org/forum/amarna/2_cmndmts_book_of_the_dead.html. [Online] 2012, 16-March. [Cited: 2012, 16-March.]
131. **Joseph Murphy, PH.D., D.D.** *The Power of Your Subconscious Mind.* s.l.: The Penguin Group, 2009.
132. **Buddharakkhita, Acharya.** *The Dhammapada; the Buddha's Path to Freedom.* Kandy: Buddhist Publication Society, 2007.
133. **Riedweg, Christoph and Rendall, Steven.** *Pythagoras: His Life, Teaching, and Influence.* s.l.: Cornell University Press.
134. **Maijastina, Kahlos.** *Debate and Dialogue: Christian and Pagan Cultures C. 360-430.*
135. **Plotinus.** *Plotinus or the Simplicity of Vision.* [trans.] Michael Chase. Chicago: University of Chicago Press, 1993. pp. 20, 21.
136. **Teplitsky, Nataly.** http://www.theepochtimes.com/n2/arts-entertainment/leo-tolstoy-100-years-later-46132.html. [Online] 2010, 18-November. [Cited: 2012, 9-May.]

137. **Plato.** *Plato Complete Works.* Indianopolis: Hacket Publishing Company, Inc, 1997. p. 33.

138. **Planck, Max.** *Treatise on Thermoynamics, Third Edition Translated from the Seventh German Edition.* London: Longmans, Green & Company, 1927. p. 40.

139. **Nanamoli, Bhikkhu and Bodhi, Bhikkhu.** *The Middle Length Discourses of the Buddha.* Second Edition. Somerville: Wisdom Publications, 2001. pp. 379-395, 493-497, 1053-1067, 1058-1065.

140. **Watts, Alan.** *Eastern Wisdom and Modern Life: Collected Talks 1960-1969.* Novato: New World Library, 2006. p. 243.

141. **Pascal, Blaise.** *Pascal's Pensées.* New York: E. P. Dutton & Co., Inc., 1958.

142. **Connor, James A.** *Pascal's Wager: the man who played dice with God.* San Francisco: HarperSanFrancisco, 2006.

143. **Rongxi, Li and Guruge, Ananda W. P., [trans.].** *The Biographical Scripture of King Asoka.* Rosemead: The International Academy of Buddhism, Hsi Lai University, 2000.

144. **Marx, Karl.** *Contribution to Critique of Hegel's Philosophy of Right.* [trans.] Joseph O'Malley. Oxford: Oxford University Press, 1970.

145. **De Sade, Donatien-Alphonse-Francoise.** *Juliette the Marquis De Sade.* [trans.] Austryn Wainhouse. New York: Publishers Group West, 1968.

146. **Dyer, Wayne W.** *You'll See It When You Believe It.* New York: HarperCollins Publishers, Inc, 2001.

147. **Dhalla, Maneckji Nusservanji.** *History of Zoroastrianism.* New York: Oxford University Press, 1938. pp. 11-26.

148. **Jung, C.G.** *The Collected Works of C.G. Jung. Vol 8: The Structure and Dynamics of the Psyche. P.412 [Trans. Gerhard Adler & R. F. C. Hull.* New Jersey: Princeton University Press, 1975. p. 210.

149. **Schneider, Tammi J.** *Ancient Mespopotamian Religion.* Grand Rapids: Wm. B. Eerdmans Publishing Co, 2011.

150. **Murphy, Joseph, PH.D., D.D.** *The Power of Your Subconscious Mind.* New York: The Penguin Group, 2009. pp. 34, 64-69, 78.

151. **Bhaskarananda, Swami.** *The Essentials of Hinduism: A Comprehensive Overview of the World's Oldest Religion.* Seattle: Viveka Press, 2002. pp. 115-130.

152. **Melton, Gordon J. and Baumann, Martin, [ed.].** *Religions of the World: A Comprehensive Encyclopedia of Beliefs and Practices.* 2nd. Santa Barbara: s.n., 2010.

153. **Kramer, Samuel Noah.** *The Sumerians: Their History, Culture, and Character.* Chicago: The University of Chicago Press, 1971.

154. **Peters, F. E. and Esposito, John L.** *The Children of Abraham: Judaism, Christianity, Islam.* New Jersey: Princeton University Press, 2004.

155. **Prime, Rachor.** *Hinduism (World Religions Series).* Vancouver: Whitecap Books, 2004. p. 10.

156. **Dicarlo, Christopher W.** *How to Become a Really Good Pain in the Ass: A Critical Thinker's Guide to Asking the Right Questions.* New York: Prometheus Books, 2011. pp. 121-122.

157. **Edgell, Penny.** Atheists identified as America's most distrusted minority, according to new U of M study. *UM News.* [Online] 2006, 28-March. [Cited: 2012, 3-January.] http://www1.umn.edu/news/news-releases/2006/UR_RELEASE_MIG_2816.html.

158. **Dawkins, Richard.** *The God Delusion.* London: Bantam Press, 2006.

159. **Geza, Vermes.** *The Complete Dead Sea Scrolls in English.* London: Penguin Books, 2004. p. 14.

160. **Mitchell, Stephen.** *Gilgamesh: A New English Version.* New York: Free Press, 2004. p. 5.

161. **Ken, Johnson, Th.D.** *Ancient Seder Olam: A Christian Translation of the 2000-year-old Scroll.* 2006. p. 20.

162. **King, Leonard William.** *The Enuma Elish: The Seven Tablets of Creation.* London: Evinity Publishing Inc, 2009. pp. 6.

163. **Nard, Don, Robert, Ed B. and Kebric, B.** *Greenhaven encyclopedia of Ancient Mesopotamia.* Detroit: Greenhaven Press Gale Virtual Reference Library, 2007. pp. 46, 119-120.

164. **Sandars, N. K.** *The Epic of Gilgamesh.* London: Penguin Group, 1972. pp. 108-113. 978-0-140-44100-0.

165. **Ehrman, Bart D.** *Misquoting Jesus: the story of who changed the Bible and why.* New York: HarperCollins.

166. "*Constantine.*" Encyclopædia Britannica Online Library Edition. s.l.: Encyclopædia Britannica, 2012.

167. **Wilhelm, Joseph.** *Protestantism.* New York: Robert Appleton Company, 1911. Vol. 12.

168. **Bodanis, David.** *Electric Universe: the shocking true story of electricity.* New York: Crown Publishing Group, 2005. 1-4000-4550-9.

169. **Piyadassi, Thera.** *The Seven Factors of Enlightenment: Satta Bojjhanga. Kandy: Buddhist Publication Society, 1960.*

170. "Religions." Central Intelligence Agency. *The World Factbook 2009.* [Online] 2012, 21-June. [Cited: 2012, 21-June.] https://www.cia.gov/library/publications/the-world-factbook/fields/print_2122.html.

171. *Seneca Letters from a Stoic.* London: Penguin Group, 1969, 2004. Vol. Letter XC p171.

172. *"Bible." Funk & Wagnalls New World Encyclopedia. Web.* Ipswich: World Almanac Education Group, Inc., 2012. p. Bible.

173. *"Koran." Funk & Wagnalls New World Encyclopedia. Web.* Ipswich: World Almanac Education Group, Inc., 2012.

174. **Dyer, Wayne W.** *Real Magic: Creating Miracles in Everyday Life.* HarperCollins: s.n., 1992. p. 303.

175. **Penguin Classics.** *Seneca Letters from a Stoic.* London: Penguin Group, 1969, 2004. Vol. Letter XC p171.

176. **Hall, James Albert.** *Hypnosis: A Jungian Perspective.* New York: Guilford Press, 1989.

177. **CIA, Central Intelligence Agency.** Religions. *The World Factbook 2009.* [Online] 2012, 21-June. [Cited: 2012, 21-June.] https://www.cia.gov/library/publications/the-world-factbook/fields/print_2122.html.

178. *"Conservation of Energy." Oxford Dictionaries.* s.l.: Oxford University Press, 2010.

179. **Levy, Rick and Aronica, Lou.** *Miraculous Health: How to Heal Your Body by Unleashing the Hidden Power of.* New York: First Atria Books/Beyond Words Publishing, 2008. p. 46.

180. **Kahlos, Maijastina.** *Debate and Dialogue: Christian and Pagan Cultures C. 360-430.* Hampshire: Ashgate Publishing Limited, 2007. 978-0-7546-5713-2.

181. **Herholz, Karl, Heiss, W. D. and Herscovitch, Peter.**

NeuroPET: PET in Neuroscience and Clinical Neurology. s.l.:
Springer-Verlag Berlin Heidelberg, 2004. p. 4. 978-3540006915.

182. **Maude, Aylmer.** *The Life of Tolstoy: Later years.* London: Kess-
inger Publishing, 2007. 978-0548034170.

183. **Austin, James H.** *Zen and the Brain: Toward an Understanding of
Meditation and Consciousness.* Cambridge: Massachusetts Institute of Technology, 1999. 978-0262511094.

184. "Hypothesis." Dictionary.com Unabridged.Web: Random House,
Inc., 2014.

12174471R00104

Printed in Great Britain
by Amazon